Praise

The impact of compassion on personal relationships and business success is not always fully appreciated. In *How Did You Get Here?* Scott Montgomery brilliantly explains how combining compassion with a rigorous work ethic and a focus on helping others vaulted him to success in his corporate and personal life. The book also does a great job of emphasizing how finding and listening to mentors can help you discover your own path, while also stressing the value of coaching and mentoring others yourself when the opportunity arises.
Patricia M. DiLella | Program Manager, Kronos/ UKG Practice, Worldgate, LLC

Scott Montgomery's life is a daring adventure! His new book, *How Did You Get Here?* is a down-to-earth tale of his journey of self-discovery and the world of work. He's got boundless energy and enthusiastically tells the story of his ups and downs—from his earliest days as a stock person through the great success he's achieved at Worldgate LLC. Full of good advice and great humor, you'll enjoy reading or listening to Scott's insights and will probably find yourself reflecting on your own journey, as well.
Gretchen M. Krampf, MSOD, PCC | Process Consultant & Leadership Coach

Scott Montgomery didn't grow up with a blueprint or the financial means for creating a multimillion-dollar company, but the struggles he experienced on the way to becoming the leader of a major consulting company taught him valuable lessons about what it takes to be successful. His book, *How Did You Get Here?* provides an enthralling account of important junctures in his life and the techniques he developed for building relationships and developing the mindset necessary to achieve success. I highly recommend it to anyone looking for an off-the-beaten-path formula for success.

Debbie Karcher | K12 Technology Adviser;
Former CIO MDCPS

An inspiring, heartfelt read from start to finish. Scott Montgomery's narrative brings many powerful life and leadership lessons into clear view as he details his journey from an unfocused youth into an effective, purpose-driven adult. The stories and insights revealed in *How Did You Get Here?* provide a map to improving the ability to achieve goals and get more out of life.

Ellen Fulton, MCC | Coach and Coach Educator,
Washington Coaching Group

What does it take to develop the mindset and focus to perform at your peak and achieve success—in your business and personal life? *How Did You Get Here?* by Scott Montgomery provides an up close and personal story of how he managed to accomplish this by combining a high regard for developing and nurturing personal relationships with developing the mental skills necessary to perform at your best. The result is a masterpiece of both the self-actualization and leadership genres—one well worth a place on your bookshelf.

Sara Rund, ACC | Senior Executive Strategy & Transformational Leadership

How Did You Get Here? shows how you can create success in both your personal and business worlds by paying attention to your relationships and being prepared for opportunities when they come up. Scott Montgomery writes passionately and engagingly about how his insatiable curiosity about people—together with his unrelenting thirst for improvement—led to him changing his fortunes from humble beginnings to becoming the founder of a highly successful corporation. I highly recommend this inspiring book.

Paul King | Former Fortune 100 CIO

Scott Montgomery's story is an inspirational journey that proves to all that one can overcome perceptions, misgivings, and obstacles real or imagined. His book *How Did You Get There* is a must-read for all that have yet to find their passion and way. His inspiring story relates to so many that have just been reluctant to take risks and have yet to take their first step towards a productive future. There is a path forward; Scott found it his way and has proven that there are many ways to achieve goals. There is no one way to gain success, but as you read Scott's story, you will readily realize that hard work and grit will provide a path so that success can be achieved. His cooperate to graduate attitude towards business as well as life itself is truly an inspiration and should be a model to all.

William D. Lublin | LTC US Army (Ret)

If you want to learn how to follow the conventional path to success, don't read *How Did You Get Here?* by Scott Montgomery. On the other hand, if you want to read a book that can inspire and teach how to overcome a humble business start to become a business leader, this book should be at the top of your list. While Montgomery offers a variety of tips and techniques for staying focused, building relationships, and developing a winning mindset in order to help his readers reach peak performance, his road to the top was anything but traditional. The book chronicles how help from mentors and a drive to succeed changed Montgomery from an unmotivated, undereducated young man to a leader in the business world.

Linda Misegadis, CPP, CPM, CCM, IPMA-CP | Chief Government Strategist, UKG, Inc.

Most self-help books, however helpful the message, can be a bit of a chore to read. *How Did You Get Here?* was the opposite! What a refreshing and relatable story about what truly drives success. The author, Scott Montgomery, skillfully weaves his advice for building leadership and relationship skills from real world lessons learned in his journey from a chaotic childhood to a worker bee with little education to his rise as an accomplished business leader. The book was impactful, heartfelt, and enjoyable to read.

Justin Zubrick | Client Services, Worldgate, LLC

GAIN MORE WISDOM FOR YOUR JOURNEY.

Follow Scott Montgomery's latest insights, tools, and teachings at **HowDidYouGetHere.com**, as you pursue your goals and forge your own unique path to greater success.

▶ **Sign up to stay driven.**

Visit **HowDidYouGetHere.com** and download our **FREE** goal-setting guide — to help you get to your next milestone.

HOW DID YOU GET HERE?

Lessons of Unconventional Success

Scott Montgomery, ACC

Leaders
Press

Leaders
Press

ISBN 978-1-63735-138-3 (pbk)
ISBN 978-1-63735-139-0 (e-book)

SIMON &
SCHUSTER

Print Book Distributed by Simon & Schuster
1230 Avenue of the Americas
New York, NY 10020

Library of Congress Control Number: 2021920750

*This book is dedicated to my wife Katelyn,
my children Evan, Teddy, and Phoebe, my parents
Judy and Dennis, and my deceased brother Dan.*

Contents

Introduction

"I didn't get there by wishing for it or hoping for it, but by working for it." —Estée Lauder

When I meet people and share what I do for work, I understand that they make certain assumptions about me—that my entrepreneurial success is the result of an Ivy League education and the homes I live in are the result of growing up with family money. That I started from *something*, and success is something I've always enjoyed.

Those who knew me in my younger years would laugh at these assumptions as they couldn't be farther from the truth. People who've known me throughout my entire life recognize that my journey did not start as some valiant march *toward* success, rather as an escape from chaos. Every milestone in my career—from my first job, to my first car, to moving away from my hometown—were attempts to run away from the kind of upbringing that typically doesn't end being surrounded by a happy and loving family, owning multiple homes, all supported by a thriving business.

But that's exactly where I ended up.

Today, I am proud to say that I am the co-founder and Chief Customer Officer of Worldgate LLC, a technology consulting firm. We provide K-12 school districts with solutions that help them achieve their Information Technology (IT) goals. As I write this book, we have engaged hundreds of customers who have spent upward of $60 million to work with our stellar team.

I am not just an entrepreneur. I am also a person who spent his early days trying to make order out of chaos, who almost lost himself completely in his early twenties, and who bounced back and began an ascent by climbing the corporate ladder at Verizon.

I don't know how many people in senior management, or those starting award-winning companies have experienced the uncertainty I've known. Rather, I find they were often prepared for a bright future by growing up in a steady home and graduating from a great college. That's OK with me. I am pleased when people learn that I've followed an unconventional path to success.

I am pleased and thrilled to hear the same question, asked over and over, after I explain my background:

"How did you get here?"

How did I get here?

Well, let me tell you.

This book intends to capture how I turned a childhood of escape attempts around and worked towards success and happiness in my adulthood. To me, "success" and "happiness" are the same.

You know the old saying, "It's a marathon, not a sprint?" Achieving success was more than a marathon—it was an Ironman. Along the way, I may or may not have been disqualified during the Ironman, in the literal sense. But disqualifications, bad habits, and other moments of havoc can always provide opportunities for positivity and growth if one chooses to see them that way. Through the good, the bad, and the ugly, I've learned that I have the choice to maximize my potential and make lemonade out of lemons. I've had to refine my leadership skills and overcome some bad habits along the way, and it all began with *making the choice* to see the lemonade in the lemons.

As you are reading this book, know that you have these same options. You will learn what choices you might make that will carry you forward, toward the success that you seek for yourself, your career, and your family. It doesn't matter where you come from or where you want to go. It's really about embracing that you have the choice to move ahead, toward your destination, with determination and a smile on your face.

Who Is This Book For?

As I came into adulthood, married, and began a family, I realized that the life of an employee, working until retirement at the age of sixty-five, would never satisfy my desires. I wanted more. The corporate ladder only has so many rungs, and I felt I wasn't qualified to achieve certain levels of advancement within the corporate vortex. I also wanted to—*had* to—leave my own mark on the world.

Does this sound familiar with your own intentions for your life? Then you're reading the right book.

I want to help any curious, driven young person or budding entrepreneur in the same position I was in so many decades ago. Perhaps you're unsure about where you are heading, but certain you're destined to go *somewhere*.

Early on I discovered I could escape my situation by earning money. When I began working in high school, I was already a leader in my own life, even though I didn't identify my mindset with leadership at the time. Though not a stellar student, I was ambitious and personable and made the choice to forge a better life for myself. I'd discovered the potential that holding down a job brought me. I took that opportunity and ran with it.

All of the lessons that I share in this book—from the importance of goal-setting to how to communicate with others—are what I have been learning from those earliest opportunities and the many others that followed. Over time, applying my natural strengths and developing new skills, I have become an effective leader and in extraordinary measure, a happy and successful person. The same can be true for you, too.

An Unconventional Guide to Success

This is not a conventional guide to entrepreneurship because I've never approached my career in a conventional way. At an early age, my life took me on an alternate path. I did not have a formal higher education to get me further in life, but I have found I can always rely on my ability to build and properly manage relationships. Business relationships don't have to be stiff, cold, or rigid. In fact, if you try to separate your business life from your personal life, you might find yourself falling short of meeting your full potential. Don't believe me? What if I told you that the president and co-founder of Worldgate, LLC is my wife, Katelyn?

Don't be afraid to open your heart and embrace your humanity as you begin this journey. People want to connect. They will be more receptive to what you have to say and more willing to help you reach success. Trust me. I didn't succeed in a vacuum. No person is an island.

I am excited to be sharing what I have learned about relationships, communication, and skills that I've found useful throughout my journey. I've blended practical knowledge with personal stories that stand as examples. You are welcome to apply the advice I'm offering. I hope this book serves as part of my legacy and I'm honored that you've chosen to pick it up.

This book was written at a pivotal time in my life, in a period of great grief. Recently, I'd lost my brother, Dan. His death was unexpected. Our relationship was a whirlwind of highs and lows and he was the only person who'd had a front-row seat to our crazy childhood. Only after his passing did I realize that, subconsciously, I'd been looking forward to our senior years as a time when we might reminisce on all we had been through and how we'd become the people we were meant to be. Dan was the first person to teach me that success is not achieved as a solitary pursuit and I can trace so much of what I have learned about relationships back to him. I will never have a chance to tell him how much I've learned from him, and I miss him dearly.

Writing this book has been a part of my grieving process. My brother never got the opportunity to share his story, and I will not let that opportunity pass me by. It's important to me to create a legacy for my children and their children. I also want to offer a guide for future generations of entrepreneurs. This is my time to pass the torch.

Young people who spend their childhoods escaping chaos by creating chaos must not count themselves out. Even those privileged often feel discouraged, living in a society where they are told they *must* be the best at everything they do, that they have to go to college in order to get a great nine-to-five job, and that is how they'll be successful.

I am a product of my upbringing. Despite what life handed me at an early age—a chaotic and self-destructive childhood, lack of credentials, and having little formal education—I have persevered. I've worked hard, taken risks, and engaged and built long-standing relationships with people. My experiences suggest that there's more than one single path in life. Your path, like mine, might be a winding one that will lead to *your* happiness. You can have a rich and fulfilling life by not taking the traditional path, as long as you have curiosity, look for the tools you need, build, your skills and attend to your relationships. If I can help in this exploration by sharing my stories, and lessons learned, I'll be happy with what I have written. I appreciate and embrace my unconventional path. May this book be a guide for you to do the same.

How to Use This Book:

In each chapter of this book, I share stories about my experiences and the relationships that I have built and benefitted from, throughout my life's journey. As you read, you may notice similarities to your own experiences.

At the end of each chapter, I pose five questions, offered to guide you in your personal exploration of how relationships and experiences are building your success.

Do you like to work with a journal? Take time to reflect and write about what arises.

Or you can download a PDF of these prompts from my website, www.howdidyougethere.com. You can print these out to hand-write, or use the fillable-feature to capture and save your insights on your computer.

If you have a coach or thought-partner, share what you are discovering as you do these exercises.

All the best on your unconventional journey—personally and professionally,

—*Scott*

1
Partypships

> *"Alone we can do so little; together we can do so much."* —Helen Keller

My mother learned of my brother's passing before I did. But my mother wasn't the person to tell me, though she'd tried calling me several times. I was in my office, deep in the "no-phone zone," completely oblivious to everything outside the room. I might have gone through the entire afternoon in this headspace If my wife, Katelyn hadn't gotten ahold of me. Katelyn had spoken to my mother and knew she could find me in the office. After she called the second time, I answered.

"Call your mother," Katelyn said. She didn't want to be the person to break the devastating news and she thought I should hear it from my mother. *"Call your mother, now!"* I didn't understand the urgency until Katelyn broke down in tears and panic. Her impactful words, *"Call your mother. Dan died!"* are forever etched in my heart.

Thus began a new chapter in our story as a couple. This chapter is one of many, as our partnership has overcome numerous personal and professional obstacles, as well as milestones we've celebrated. Many of the accomplishments—and much of the leadership advice I'll share—is made possible because of my partnership with Katelyn. She has been a source of support since I first met her as an intern in 1995, and she's been the string to my kite ever since.

The first time we discussed the idea of our relationship being like "a string to a kite" was in 2017. Katelyn's father had invited us to attend a charity dinner with Jack Nicklaus, one of the greatest golfers of all time. The event was beautifully planned, and each of the twenty-five attendees got to have ample time to chat with the legend himself. Katelyn and I were so humbled to talk to Jack and his wife, who were no strangers to the balance that a married couple must have if they go into business together. Jack's wife, Barbara, is known as "The First Lady of Golf," running the Nicklaus Children's Health Care Foundation for years. As the four of us shared stories about our experiences balancing personal and professional responsibilities, Katelyn leaned over towards me and said, *"Sometimes I worry, Scott, that I'm too much a string to your kite."*

Worry? I never saw this dynamic in our relationship as something she had to worry about. What is a kite if it doesn't have a string to navigate it? It is just fabric without a string, doomed to end up crashing into a tree, getting completely lost in the clouds, or never taking off in the first place.

Through everything I have learned, every risk that I have taken in business, and every celebration of life and family, Katelyn has been the steady string to my kite. I want to articulate how important she is to me as my wife, the mother of our children, and as my business partner. We own a business and have a family together, and I believe how we interact with one another, as *"kite and string,"* brings us success in these partnerships.

Moments of Serendipity

Katelyn and I met shortly after she was hired as an intern at Verizon. I had just moved to Virginia for my job and was starting to "clean the slate" after my earlier years of self-destruction and irresponsibility. I had a bit of a reputation for having "street smarts." I had been given a special assignment in Virginia Beach in the summer of 1994, recognized for the hard work I'd done and the relationships I'd made, I was promoted and moved to Arlington later that year. My trajectory through the management ranks at Verizon seemed shorter than most.

Meanwhile, Katelyn was studying for her MBA and the curriculum included an internship. Brilliant and well-educated, she's always been a perfect example of what it means to have "book smarts."

One of my coworkers knew I was interested in her and couldn't help but tease me. "She's way out of your league," she told me. I knew there was truth to what she was saying, but that didn't stop me from putting myself out there. I was young and cocky. Fortunately, that didn't bother Katelyn. After we attended her first staff meeting at Verizon, we went on our first date to Outback Steakhouse.

Before I moved to Virginia, I had this vision of myself, playing the field in my new neighborhood and approaching personal relationships and big decisions casually. I was more interested in getting a dog and a tattoo than I was in getting married. I saw myself as a young guy who had racked up a bunch of credit card debt and was trying to turn things around. Four months into dating, I quickly realized I would be foolish to let her slip away. I was going to have to get a dog, a tattoo, and a *girlfriend*.

One evening, a few months into our courtship, we sat in a booth inside Whitlow's on Wilson, both prepared to have a serious conversation. I was going to ask her to be my exclusive girlfriend. She was going to break up with me. Lucky for both of us, Katelyn came to this conversation with control, empathy, and an ability to communicate effectively. She knows how to meet people where they are and that is key for good communication.

At the table that night, we both mentioned how we had something to talk about. She let me talk first. She met me where I was—a young guy who wasn't going to be able to recover if she went first and bruised my ego by slowing down our relationship. That forethought saved our relationship. She was only breaking up with me because she didn't think I was taking the relationship seriously. She thought I was going to try to string her along. She navigated the conversation with empathy and was able to see where I really was within our budding relationship. We ended up dating exclusively and getting married four years later.

We might have gotten married sooner, but I had some catching up to do. I wanted to get to a place where I felt comfortable and financially stable enough to start a family. I'd gotten the dog, the tattoo, and my finances were getting in order. Once I'd paid off my credit card debt and my credit score recovered, I bought my first townhouse. I intended it as a place for Katelyn and me to start our married life together. For Katelyn, this was a struggle as she needed to redirect her notion of wanting to buy her first house as a married couple. Katelyn had always pictured buying a house *with* her husband.

I bought *my* first house because I worked hard to recover from my earlier poor decisions and there were many stars aligning in my career and personal life. I was beginning to feel successful. Katelyn and I got married, sharing that first house and making it *ours*, relishing in times with new friends and loving our dog, Lexi. Within two years, the Northern Virginia real estate market had taken off and our townhouse had almost doubled in value. We decided it was time to sell.

Katelyn and I looked at roughly forty different houses, but none of them was *the one*. Walking through those houses was exhausting and we were spent, discouraged and about to give up. After viewing several houses in one area, we decided to take a different route back to our townhouse. We drove through a beautiful neighborhood and there was an open house where a great realtor—and now a family friend, Annie—was working. As we contemplated the features and affordability of the house, and other personal interests, Annie told us there was another house in the neighborhood, soon coming on the market, so we scheduled a showing. People were knocking on the doors trying to get a tour, as we were looking at it for the first time—that's just how hot the real estate market was.

Katelyn and I toured the house, growing more and more confident that this was *the one*. As we turned the corner into the family room, Katelyn saw a large picture of a sailboat—the same exact picture that we had in our townhouse. Katelyn's lip started quivering. She didn't have to say anything. I saw this and knew it as a sign that this was going to be our forever home. The homeowner was there that day and we chatted about the market. He took a shine to our life's story and gave us three days to sell our townhouse in order to make a non-contingent offer on his house. Three days...and we did it! That's how we found ourselves moving into a five-bedroom, 4 bath, 4500 square foot home in the very early days of our marriage. We are still here, twenty years later, creating memories and raising our three children.

Rarely would one make real estate decisions based on a picture of a sailboat, but I was present in that moment and saw what was in front of me: serendipity. So many small moments have happened, to be where I was and get to the place where Katelyn and I are now. I've had to learn to tap into these moments, notice and embrace them, while letting the wind steer my kite. Katelyn, grounded, with string in hand, has been navigating beside me, making sure my kite is not flying off in the wrong direction for us and our family.

Katelyn met me at a time when I felt like I was picking up the pieces of an irresponsible phase of my life. Although she had pictured herself buying her first house *with* her husband, she acknowledged the importance of my kite moving through that process. I needed to sign that deed to my *own* house to feel that my personal progress had reached a successful outcome and was complete. She saw where I was, accepted where I was, and let me catch up to myself. Having resolved the financial chaos I had created for myself in my early twenties, we were now able to move forward.

Together, we make a great team. Even before we decided to go into business together, we operated and communicated with the expectation that we are going to be married until the day we take our final breaths. We refuse to take the path that leads many couples to let their communication fall by the wayside or put off issues until embroiled in a nasty divorce. Strategically, "divorce" is a word never to be used in our home. Being proactive in our communications and thinking carefully about how to best approach each other takes a lifetime of learning, growing, and making mistakes. We have worked on that foundation from the day we became committed as a couple.

Katelyn's naturally in tune with other people—their wants, needs, and egos. She has a strong grasp on how her actions may be perceived by others, and she *cares* about that. She sees what I don't see, as naturally as the string to my kite. When I start flying too high and close to the sun, she reels me in—*just enough*—to stabilize and not stifle my growth. Her steadiness ensures that we get everything done by executing many of the finer details needed in our shared vision for family, business, and our lives together. Committed, we are able to face anything and everything. We respect one another, provide space for each other, and have learned how our individual strengths fit together as a whole. All of this work has been beneficial and essential to how we balance our business and personal relationships. I couldn't imagine partnering, in business or in life, with anyone else.

Everything for Our Children

We bought a house with five bedrooms, a set-up rarely chosen by a young couple without any children. Our vision for a home, filled with children, didn't begin to take form until about four years later. It wasn't for a lack of trying. We didn't enter our marriage with the expectation we'd have fertility issues. No one signs up for the grief of a miscarriage. But with every month that went by, as we attempted starting our family, Katelyn and I grew closer. I discovered the immense strength and determination that she possesses. I saw how forgiving she could be as I stumbled along, trying to be of comfort, offering my sometimes reckless or clumsy compassion.

In time, we've had three children. Our eldest son, Evan, and our twins, Teddy and Phoebe were born just over two years apart. Three babies, and paying for a five-bedroom house, set up a hefty new goal. This was going to get expensive. It shook us into realizing that we had to take our careers to the next level. The way we looked at our relationship and careers completely shifted in 2008.

The year Katelyn and I had "three kids under three," our financial planner suggested that beyond funding retirement, we also needed to start thinking about saving for college. Educating three kids through university could easily cost hundreds of thousands of dollars. Should our children decide to pursue that educational path, Katelyn and I don't want to put limits on which schools they may want to attend or have them worry about how to pay their college expenses—we want them to be able to focus on their studies.

When I realized how much we needed to earn and save to provide for these scenarios, I realized I was going to have to change things up. At that point, my getting a college degree might pull me up a few rungs on the corporate ladder, but that would require more time away from the family and I knew the corporate job has a ceiling. Entrepreneurship was the only way I was going to generate the income needed to build the life I wanted, and we needed to provide for our family. I started exploring options.

At that time, Katelyn was earning a good salary and benefits, as she'd stayed in her corporate job. I considered getting my license and becoming a realtor. Living in the DC metro-area, during a boom market, selling real estate could afford me the opportunity to earn an unlimited income and have a flexible schedule that would help me tend to our young family's needs. Katelyn, with her steady hand on the string, was able to hold down our financial fort. In case the market crashed and all the wind died beneath me, she'd at least provide a salary that could support us. She held the string to one of the highest kites I set to fly.

I got my Virginia salesperson license and have maintained an active license every year since. I have loved selling real estate, making new friends, in clients and across the industry, while being challenged differently, as a salesperson. I was making good money, a name for myself in the local market, and was invited to become an investor/partner in a new brokerage, Keller Williams, that was seeding start-up offices in Northern Virginia. I found success selling to first time buyers and was *thrilled* when I scored my first

$2 million listing. I felt real estate was broadening my emerging business strengths. I could leverage my relational skills and I was generating the financial success I needed to meet the demands of supporting our growing family.

Katelyn and I set up Worldgate LLC when I began investing in real estate. It was established as a partnership, with Katelyn as President, holding 51% interest to my 49% interest. When you're a realtor, you operate as a contractor rather than an employee, and having our limited liability company, I was also able to stay open to other opportunities, too.

I still had active connections in my corporate network as I intentionally stayed in touch with them as time went by. Over dinner one night, I was asked if I could spare some time from my real estate practice and consult with them, bringing my experience from earlier corporate days to their public sector mission. It wasn't long before my consulting work expanded and I found myself pivoting from just real estate into working with corporate clients in a new way I had not considered before.

We'd certified the business in Virginia and had the foresight to register it as Women Owned, intending to be able to consider women-owned business opportunities. Eventually, more opportunities in corporate consulting surfaced, and we were prepared. Worldgate was becoming an IT consulting firm that would specialize in supporting the public sector, specifically the

K-12 education market. We would support the business system implementations and staffing needs.

Katelyn's kite strings were crucial as I focused on moving our company into the consulting services arena. I continued selling real estate, opportunistically, while focusing on creating a broader strategy for Worldgate. There were emerging opportunities that would allow Katelyn and me to achieve everything we wanted in our careers. We would be able to live the lifestyle we wanted *and* be there for our family. We could be home for our kids at any time.

It was settled. I would nurture and expand our client relationships while directing the vision for the business. Katelyn, as President, would run our internal operations for finance and HR. My sales kite could fly high and her deep experience in corporate operations would keep the family and our company steady. Who knew then that Worldgate would eventually achieve recognition as INC. Magazine's "5000 Fastest Growing Companies," the Brava Award, Fairfax County Public Schools Honor Roll, and the Washington Post's "Top Workplaces 2022."

Intentionally Balancing Partnerships

Not every couple considers going into business together. Not every couple *should* consider going into business together. If I had attempted to start this business with anyone else, it would have been virtually impossible to maintain the balance between a professional and personal relationship. But the skills Katelyn and I have learned together are skills that make our success possible.

A lot of what we do as parents, in life and as business partners is done with *intention*. Whether it's scheduling a date night or sitting down to have a conversation about something that is bothering us, we work to think clearly and be present in how we approach our relationship. Parenting is a whirlwind. All of a sudden, you blink, and your children are teenagers, asking to borrow the car.

Entrepreneurship is a whirlwind, too. It is dynamic and when you are intentional, carving out the correct roles and responsibilities for the partnership, communicating and striving to work well together, you can achieve the goals you set for yourselves. Whether you are the kite or you are the string, lean into your role.

Maybe you'll be fortunate enough to find that person who partners as well with you. What matters most is that when you find someone who complements your strengths, be sure to stay present within your relationship. Embrace those moments of clarity and serendipity and you will go great places together.

Questions for You

1. How are you like the Kite? How are you like the String?
2. What values do you and your partner share?
3. How are you intentional with your partner?
4. Why is partnering important for your success?
5. When do you intentionally check in with your partner?

2
Relationships

"The business of business is relationships; the business of life is human connection." —Robin S. Sharma

Dan died unexpectedly in New York City on September 25, 2019. He was only 54 and my brother's passing was a shock to our family and his friends. Uncle Dan was a favorite of the kids, Evan, Teddy, and Phoebe, always enjoyed our many shared holidays—like going to NYC for Thanksgiving and taking in the Macy's Parade. Dan had been with us in Virginia for the Christmas holidays in 2018. He and I'd ended our visit cordially, but in a bit of conflict, having differing points of view regarding some of our shared responsibilities. We didn't really communicate for months and my reply to the "Happy Birthday" text he'd sent to me in late August, was answered with a brief "Thanks!"

A month later, he was gone. I was catapulted into the whirlwind of funeral arrangements, dealing with the numerous and necessary legal issues that required immediate attention, as well as being the only remaining son, consoling my mom and dad. Katelyn, though heartbroken, brought her strong and steady presence, caring for our kids' emotional and physical needs, as well as supporting me as I wound through the maze of this tragedy. There is a sense of order that she gave me that in turn offered some stability—the compression of time one has to prepare for a funeral, arranging for the service, coordinating communications, accommodating arriving company, and planning for a reception after the service. I was exhausted, and still in shock, when we arrived at our church for the Mass.

Pulling into the church parking lot, I wasn't surprised to see how many cars were already there. Katelyn and I, having three children in local schools and sports, have many acquaintances and we've built some deep connections, as families. Our company, Worldgate, is based in Reston, Virginia and our employees, vendors and our clients reside within a three-state radius. Dan lived in Manhattan, but our mother lived in Virginia and she struggled with travel so we decided to hold services there, as a convenience for her. Several of Dan's friends had also travelled south to be there. These people were the ones who run like a *golden thread* through our lives. As I looked around the church, and reflected on the service, I became more aware of the many types of relationships I'd developed over the years and felt great comfort that so many were present.

What *did* surprise and touched me deeply was seeing Julie in the church. I'd met Julie two decades earlier, at Verizon, when I was given a special assignment in Virginia Beach to work with her. My interest and belief in the power of asking for what I wanted nudged me to take a chance. I recalled pulling her aside, saying,

"If you ever have a job opening, please consider hiring me," and handed her my resume. It wasn't too many months later that she extended me a tremendous offer and I moved to Arlington, Virginia.

Back then, she was a bit of a 'guardian angel' to me, offering suggestions about where I might want to live and places I could go, as a single guy in a new town. She also mentored me, connecting me with *her* network and teaching me about leadership, management, as well as how to develop more self-control so I could succeed. Julie saw my potential and gave me the opportunity to help her launch a new digital services help desk for internal Verizon employees. Her belief in me was one of the reasons I was able to move up the rungs of the corporate ladder more rapidly.

Even after heading off to different jobs, we continued to stay in touch. She and I have developed one of those relationships where, although time passes, nothing seems to change between us. We met up for lunch a few weeks after Dan's funeral and got a chance to talk about our professional experiences and our friendship. I was able to tell her how much I'd learned from her, twenty years ago, how I appreciated her continuing support, and for *still* being my guardian angel.

Networking

Truth is, I probably would not have had Julie as a mentor if I hadn't taken a chance by directly expressing an interest in working for her during the early days of a temporary work assignment. I discovered at an early age that there are many types of relationships that you can nurture and maximize, on the personal *and* professional level.

Another of my early bosses was a high school classmate's mother. She knew of me through our community and hired me to work for her. I was barely eighteen. It's another example of one not ever knowing when there will be a person *you know*, or a person *they know*, who might kick-start your career.

I have found that being interested in people and curious about what I can learn from them opens great possibilities. What would you like to know about the work that they do? What can they share with you—on skills required, expectations, and pathways to engagement? If you want to have relationships with the leaders in your company or community, go find those people and foster connections.

Invite them to have coffee, pay for the refreshments, and don't be afraid to tell them what you are interested in learning. Appreciate the time and information they share with you and acknowledge it. Ask if there is anything you could do for them. That's the way to build social capital in your network. It won't always work, but it's a lot more effective than sitting around, waiting for your next opportunity to fall from the sky. If you don't ask for what you want in your life, you're not going to get it. Ask for it.

I carried this knowledge with me when I got my first corporate job at Bell Atlantic (now Verizon). Although I was making decent money, I knew I needed to meet people, make connections, and form relationships to build my network within the company. In my Scott-style, I just went for it. There are probably several former Verizon secretaries who'd still twitch today, hearing the sound of my voice. I was tenacious, my pursuit was intense, and I'd say now that I let few boundaries get in my way if I had an opportunity to connect.

"*I'll buy!*" I would offer, over and over. With enough persistence, I was often granted the time, whether for lunch or a quick office visit. My tenacity paid off, and my network grew from early on. Of course, not everyone accepted my request to connect, but I still went for it. I am not one to get easily discouraged, and that trait has kept me whole. I had an inherent ability to determine the value of the interaction and whether to pursue it. Fortunately for me, there were enough people in senior management who took the time to meet with me that my career was never stifled by those who hid behind closed doors.

"It's not what you know, it's who you know."

People say that your early relationships—the ones that you have with your parents, siblings, and other family members—directly influence the relationships you'll form as an adult. Your family-of-origin is your first "team" experience and the workplace is where we bring our "earlier selves." Sometimes people will act in ways that relate to their birth order, or how they have been perceived in those earlier systems. I'm not a psychologist, but I am curious about human dynamics. Having worked in corporate settings as well as in entrepreneurial sales for many years, I've met all kinds of people. What I can tell you is that by developing greater awareness and nurturing my relationships, I've grown my networks and this is the core secret to my personal and professional success.

Some folks see working with the people they know *"at work"* as only transactional, all dollar signs and signatures. Or that forming friendships, for social reasons, won't influence their success in business. And not every person you meet is going to become a friend. I have many acquaintances, and I even have to manage relationships with some folks that I don't particularly share similar interests with. Yet, I have found that, through my interactions with others, I build 'social capital.' That comes from giving and receiving, supporting, and encouraging, offering and asking for what is needed.

In my opinion, I find women are often better at this than men and we men are the worse-off for it. We tend to be more competitive and protective, should we appear vulnerable. We are less inclined to collaborate or willing to invest *spacious time* to care for our emotional wellbeing by building stronger bonds through friendships.

These friendships can be the very thing that boosts our business acumen. Friendships from my earlier years, from high school and in my twenties, continue as connections, like through-lines to that younger man. I also nurture a several-decades-long relationship with three guys I've been friends with through thick and thin. Chris, Matt, Jeff, and I make time each year for a golf weekend getaway, as well as long dinners, locally, so we can get caught-up with one another. When one of us needs a trusted space to ask for feedback and support both personally and professionally, we know we will be there for each other.

Tending to family and personal connections takes time, thoughtfulness, and effort to communicate, coordinate and host times together. Personally, I consider the return-on-investment greatly builds my social capital and contributes to the richness and successes of my life.

The primary reason I show up for work every day is because of the people I am working with. Internal and client relationships have led to some becoming friends, confidants, and even like family members. Several of them have worked with me, or I for them, over many years. In my early career, they were not put off by my limited formal education, rather they valued the qualities I brought, and efforts and relationships we share. These relationships have been built with trust by being authentic and transparent with one another, responsible and accountable to the commitments we make, and resolving conflicts when they arise. I am committed to positively influencing the lives of others.

To be great, you have to start with being good. Look for ways you can be good to the people around you.

Follow Where Fate Leads You

Pat, and her husband Frank, were in the church the day of Dan's funeral. She's been a longtime mentor and a very near and dear friend. The first time I met Pat, I had a somatic response. Some call it a "gut experience" or it might be a tingle of energy that you notice on your skin.

I'll never forget the day I met Pat. I'd been referred to her by another manager, and she agreed to meet and interviewed me, on the spot, for a position on her team. Her team's mission at Verizon was changing, ordering, and provisioning capabilities for large business customers. This was another huge opportunity for me and here I was, in an impromptu interview. Walking into her office, I got that somatic 'nudge' and felt that fate had brought us together and that we were going to be in each other's lives from that moment on. It wasn't long before an offer was extended for me to join her team as a junior manager, gathering requirements.

Weeks later, I found myself in the conference room of her Philadelphia office. There were thirty members of her team assembled in this high-rise building overlooking the Philadelphia cityscape. When Pat entered the room and walked by me to sit at the head of the table, I remember feeling her aura, that there was something different about this person. The team was debriefing the results of a personality assessment. Curiously, Pat and I were the only two people who had the same results in work ethic and style and it bonded us.

Whenever Pat would come down to the Virginia office, we'd chat about the project she had me working on, where things were headed, and what problems needed to be solved. She was generous and would often spend time, at the end of the day, diving deeply into many topics. Always extremely caring, Pat offered transparency into what was happening at higher levels of management, increasing my understanding of how the organization needed to be served and how I could network within it. With her guidance, I fine-tuned skills that would become essential in starting and leading Worldgate.

Fast-forward twenty years. Now that Pat has transitioned from her corporate IT leadership role, we are fortunate that her next career move brought her to join Worldgate. For the past few years, she has been instrumental in managing our K-12 projects, while supporting our leadership and growth strategies. She also mentors several of our mid-level managers, just like she did for me in the nineties. Honestly, I've been fortunate to enjoy her support and guidance for decades, and I still do. And the lesson: When you are offered support from someone you trust, let them guide you. You might discover that the person you meet at work, even if they are managing you, becomes part of your family, over time.

Over the many years that I have known Pat, I have also come to know her sons and husband. Our early professional connection brought greater connections and deeper relationships. Today, she and her husband

Frank Sr are also known as Aunt Pat and Uncle Frank to our children. There are many milestones in life we've shared, even that very sad day of Dan's funeral and Pat continues to be an integral part of both my and Katelyn's professional and personal lives.

In 2003, I was introduced to Mel. That internal "nudge" activated again. I paid attention to the somatic signals and made sure to lean in. I didn't have a real sense of what was at hand, but the relationship with Mel guided me to be open to synchronicity. Maybe you already know your inner guidance and the somatic signals you receive have led you to new opportunities. If you can be open to seeing where they take you, follow wherever they may lead. And when you look back over several years, you'll find you've gained so much from these people by your side and appreciate that you followed your gut. These are the relationships, I believe, that will help you learn more about who you are meant to be, in your career and in your personal life.

Over the past years, Mel has transformed my views of leadership and my framework for "partnering in business." She is a client and I have learned so much from working closely with her. Worldgate provides staffing, training, and leadership development support. Mel, in her role as leader, has fostered unwavering support from my people, in part by not drawing lines between contracted staff and full-time employees. This allows us to create a model of integrating our staff with work within her system as a cohesive entity.

In the decades that we have known each other, our paths have covered a lot of ground. We've moved through highs and lows as we've worked toward reaching common goals and addressing challenges. Long ago we established trust and have built strong communications so that we always come to a common understanding and assume positive intent.

In the summer of 2016, Mel and I were invited to speak at an annual K-12 Technology and Research Conference. Our topic: "The Power and Potential of Effective Partnering." Key to our "best practice offering" was how Mel, as the client, and Worldgate have built and maintained such a highly effective and long-lasting working relationship. We spoke to SUCCESS being built by establishing TRUST through CLARITY and COMMUNICATION. My role as Worldgate's Chief Customer Officer, is making sure that I and my team bring the skills essential to engage with the client project's technical staff, as well as meet its organizational culture's social/emotional/behavioral needs. Developing strong relational connections, being able to communicate clearly, honestly, and frequently, reduces confusion and conflicts. And, being responsible and accountable is essential for building and maintaining trust.

Our partnering model enables the embedded Worldgate team to be productive and successful, which in turn allows us to better connect with our other industry clients. While this is hard to quantify, it is invaluable. She has my gratitude. She is a leader in her industry and I value any role we've played in elevating her team's mission and success.

Mel has also encouraged my personal development and growth. She wrote a recommendation for me when I enrolled at George Mason University to become a credentialed Leadership Coach in Organizational Wellbeing. And, after many years of postponing formalizing my education, she encouraged me to enroll at the University of Virginia and I am on track to complete my B.A. in Liberal Arts in early 2023.

I am honored to call her a client and a friend. Seeing her sitting in the pew, on that difficult day of Dan's funeral, I felt greatly supported by her presence.

Who Will Be at Your Funeral?

Learning how to maintain and maximize relationships is a lifelong journey. I am still learning—every day—especially from the people who have been around me for decades. Reflecting over the years and identifying the people who have been with me on my evolving journey has opened my eyes to the personal values that they and I hold. I think about the experiences we have had, through shared struggles and perseverance, up to achievement and success. I appreciate what I have gained and insights I've been given.

Thinking about legacy tends to come when one reaches their later years. Yet no one knows at what age they might die. My brother, Dan, lived his life very much "in the moment" and it ended earlier than he or I expected. His relationships, friends who came to his funeral, and NYC Memorial are part of his legacy, just as the many memories my children have of their special times with Uncle Dan.

How might this be an opportunity to think about the people *you* are in relationship with, personally and professionally? Imagine who might be present when you pass, supporting those you care for and honoring the person you have been. Who might be a contributor to *your* legacy?

Questions for You

1. Why do you think relationships are important?
2. Who in your life is bringing you closer to success?
3. When was the last time you pursued a new relationship?
4. Where could you go to build new relationships?
5. How can new relationships support you on your path to success?

3
Habits

---

*"You'll never change your life until you change something
that you do daily. The secret to your success is found in
your daily routine."* —John C. Maxwell

As a scrawny high school sophomore, I scored a job
bagging groceries at Genuardi's, a prominent local
grocery store in the late 80s. I showed up on my first day
not meeting the criteria of my new employment. My
orientation packet had specifically stated that I needed
to wear a pressed white shirt and a necktie to work. I
didn't have either. Of course I didn't. At the time, I
relished in being a rebel, a cool kid that didn't need to
follow the rules. When I arrived for my first shift, I was
immediately put in my place.

The moment my manager saw me, he pulled me aside,
read me the rules and ultimately sent me back home.
Since I couldn't yet drive, my mother had to come back
to get me and drive me home. She helped me pick out a
white shirt, that I also had to iron, before she drove me
all the way back for "take two" of my first day at work.

Showing up an hour later, wearing the right shirt and
tie, I was given a "strike one" and warned to take things
more seriously. No more rebelling at Genuardi's for me.

The consequences of my behavior brought home the simple lesson that *you get what you give*. My disregard for the expectations of my boss resulted in me starting off on the wrong foot and being embarrassed. I needed to start earning a paycheck and I was lucky that my new boss forgave my arrogance and gave me another chance. If I was going to get what I wanted, I needed to give this a better effort.

I typically worked a four-hour shift at Genuardi's, after school and weekends. I started bagging groceries and was soon promoted to the bakery department where I was responsible for setting up the next day's baking trays with the frozen dough. I would store the racks in the risers overnight so the next day they could be baked, packaged, and shelved by the head baker.

I often found that by forming routines around these tasks, I was able to execute and check everything off my list in just a few hours. Because I got everything done so efficiently, I could use the remaining hours of my shift to explore other departments, where my friends were working, and lend a hand where extra help was needed. I was happy to have the spare time to learn more about the business and support other departments. I was able to expand my network too. However, not all good deeds go unpunished. Working in the deli section one evening, I sliced my finger wide open and had to get stitches to close the wound.

Having a regular job added structure in my life and I learned that getting to the store earlier than my starting time meant I could see my friends and punch the clock on time. My boss recognized my effort and I felt appreciated. My coworkers and store managers valued my support and rewarded me with more opportunities. I discovered that as I stuck to my routine and got work done, I felt better about myself. By the end of tenth grade, I was working four-hour weeknight shifts and all day on most Saturdays. By twelfth grade, I'd added Sundays. Working at Genuardi's those two years was foundational in my work ethic. Building good work habits, getting to know and help others while making good money for my efforts meant I was able to buy my first nice, reliable car. Showing up *ten* minutes early is a habit that I still stick with today.

Lather, Rinse, Repeat...

Growing up with little structure at home, a habit that helped me create order was making my bed every morning. I kid you not, I was probably 2 or 3 years old when I began doing this. And it is a habit I still practice every day.

My team always makes fun of me for botching this phrase in meetings, but I'll make sure to get it right on paper: *"Lather, rinse, repeat."* That's me. I'm a lather, rinse, repeat kind of guy. On Monday, I make my bed, brush my teeth, rinse the sink, work out, shower, and head to work. On Tuesday, I make my bed, brush my teeth, rinse the sink, work out, shower, and head to work. *"Lather, rinse, repeat."*

There are only so many hours in a day. With regular habits that I repeat every morning, I set myself up for a successful day. When I get to work, I make my coffee, sit down at my desk, make a plan for the day, and execute. Every day, I get to work, make my coffee, sit down at my desk, make a plan for the day, and execute. As a busy person, parent, and businessman, I continue to follow these habits because they allow me to respond to my next unpredictable task at full capacity and with balance. I'm constantly striving to work at peak performance.

Habits aren't just the tasks we do. They are the structure, routines, and patterns we create for ourselves. For me, that pattern involves showing up early, getting my pens and papers in order on my desk, and doing all of the things I need to do to work at peak performance. For you, that could look different, depending on where you want to go and what you want to do.

People often ask me, "How did *you* get here?" Well, I know I do better with structure and when I practice good habits. I read and watch news outlets, especially on social media which is usually the first to know anything, in order to stay current with the research and I continue to assess my behaviors. I surrounded myself with people who respect and support my desire to stick to these habits. I've been fortunate to have people who have lifted me up, dusted me off, and exposed me to opportunities. My habits and desire to honor relationships has allowed me to take on those new opportunities with peak performance. You want to know what that is? For me, it's how I define success.

But this wasn't always the case.

***

I didn't know that I had to apply for college. For many people, applying to college or trade school is an important adult goal. Setting a goal is a *first step* and must be followed with a series of efforts to complete the necessary steps to succeed in attaining the goal of acceptance and admission.

The pressure of thinking beyond high school didn't set in until late in my senior year. I had little guidance at home, and no one in my high school invested the time to help me through the application process. I don't know that I ever met with a guidance counselor unless I was in trouble for being disruptive. No one was asking, *"Scott, what's next for you? What is your plan, post high school?"* These were definitely not questions being posed by adults, teachers, peers, or myself when I was in high school.

I remember going to visit Delaware County Community College for an Orientation Day. I remember jumping on the opportunity because I wanted to get excused from a day of high school classroom drudgery, not because I wanted to learn about their programs. On the bus ride, my friends told me that they'd never be going to DCCC. That likely they wouldn't even stay this close to home. They had aspirations for far greater opportunities like going out of state altogether for college. I remember thinking to myself, *"How do they even know how to think like that?"*

My parents and I were so disengaged from my school and I never was encouraged to look past graduating high school. The expectation was that I would go and get a job. After the community college visit, I started thinking maybe I'd go there for a year, improve my grades and transfer to one of the four-year colleges that my friends were all aspiring to attend. It didn't quite happen that way.

In high school, I had a reputation for being an uninterested, chaotic, disruptive and loudmouth student. I remember during my high school graduation rehearsal ceremony practice, a teacher I had never had a class with grabbed my arm aggressively and pulled me aside. Nowadays, he would have gotten in trouble for the grip he had on my arm. He growled quietly in my ear, *"If you mess up this graduation ceremony, I will personally hold your diploma. You'll be back next year. You will fail and won't graduate. Get your damn act together."*

This wasn't even a teacher who knew me personally, but my reputation around the school compelled him to get in front of me. I fell in line with the teacher's wishes, high five'd a buddy of mine on the podium during our actual ceremony, and graduated by the skin of my teeth. If I could, I would take those years back for a do-over. In hindsight, I would have preferred to take my education more seriously.

***

How to Break a Bad Habit

Admittedly, I developed a few bad habits over those early years. I smoked a lot of cigarettes back then, too. It wasn't a new habit, unfortunately. Before I could even spell "cigarette," I would light my parents' old butts, right out of the dirty ashtray, and pretend to smoke them when they weren't around. It officially became a habit when I was smoking at my high school bus stop, at night walking the dog around the neighborhood, and when I hung around with my friends. As we know today, smoking doesn't set you up for peak performance like good habits do. And, as any smoker knows, getting *out* of this nicotine habit is not easy.

Once I acknowledged that smoking was slowly killing me, I knew I needed to quit. The addiction had a strong hold, and there were many failed attempts before I found success. At first, I replaced the habit of smoking with working out. I would go for a run at night when I wanted a cigarette. The next morning, I would feel great—until I got to the bus stop to go to school and smoked cigarettes. At a party, thinking I was cool, I'd smoke more cigarettes. The next time I wanted to have a cigarette, I'd go for a run again. I had a taste of what it took to replace this bad habit with a good one, but it took me years to replace it completely.

After starting my job at Verizon, I was motivated to stop smoking because I was viewed differently by my coworkers when I went outside for a smoke break. It was in the early nineties, when cigarette smoking was becoming taboo. Hanging around out in front of the corporate offices, inhaling a cigarette, didn't hold me in the most professional light with leaders and coworkers. Plus, I would stink for hours when I got back to my desk.

I started by moving my habit to weekends only. I would work out religiously all week, feel better and better with each passing day. Then I would go out on Saturday night, drink with my friends, *reward* myself by buying a pack of cigarettes, and smoke the whole thing that night. Not surprisingly, I would feel crappy all day Sunday. Laying out my clothes for the next workday, washing my car, or getting my act together just didn't happen. I didn't have the energy to think about habits, much less follow through with them. And because I didn't follow through, I showed up to work on Monday bleary-eyed and unable to work at peak performance.

I liked the positive reception from my coworkers when I stopped smoking during the week. I liked how I felt throughout the week when I was working out instead of smoking. After a short while, I moved this nasty habit to every other weekend. Every other Sunday after I smoked, I still felt awful. Every other Sunday after I didn't smoke, I felt better and completed all the tasks that allowed me to work at peak performance. When you're in the throes of addiction, you don't always want to acknowledge it. Fortunately, I was able to.

Habits are generally composed of three steps: a cue that signals you should begin the habit, a routine that *is* the habit, and a reward you receive for executing the habit.

This formula applies to good and bad habits. When I had a smoking habit, the cues were everywhere—a drink with the buddies, a free minute at the bus stop, the sunset. The routine was smoking the cigarette, and the reward that I felt was the relief that smokers feel when their body receives the nicotine it was craving. To quit, I recognized some of those same cues as a sign to start exercising, have a glass of water, or just do anything else that wasn't smoking a cigarette. The reward was much greater when I turned to these habits. I didn't feel unhealthy and, eventually, I didn't feel the craving to have more nicotine.

I started smoking only once a month and finally after a few years quit altogether. In time, I started to spend Sunday evenings getting myself ready for the week ahead and that helped me succeed.

And, even better, at the same time my career started to take off. This was not entirely due to the break from my bad habit, but I'm sure my colleagues saw me in a better light when I was at my desk and not outside inhaling pollutants. I was definitely working at peak performance which helped my corporate trajectory into management. By the time I was in my mid-twenties, I began to truly understand the impact of how habits could create structure in my chaotic world.

The former politician and Olympic track and field athlete Jim Ryun once said, *"Motivation is what gets you started. Habit is what keeps you going."* Habits allow our brains to run on autopilot and at peak performance. A small shift in habit can be life-changing since the incremental improvement compounds every day that you make that better choice. Replacing bad habits with good ones helped me start to recognize the power of my decisions and actions.

Habits and Drive Accomplish Goals

When my kids read this chapter, they are bound to be shocked by my story, or maybe they'll roll their eyes. The importance of habits and how to form them are lessons that I strive to pass on to my kids as well. As early as they were capable, they started to rotate weekly between three chores: dishes, caring for the dog, and laundry/trash collection. They were assigned for the week and they would rotate on Sundays to keep their attention on learning the chores themselves, but also the habit of having chores and getting their work done. Further, some are more intense than others. Just like in real life, you have to adjust and adapt your habits based on your schedules and what is demanded of you.

I started teaching them habits early because I want them to learn the same lessons I learned at Genuardi's, Verizon, and in life. I want them to have life skills and be self-sufficient as well as create for them a work ethic that helps them maximize their potential. I'm consistently reminding them that if they get the chores done, the rest of the day is theirs. God only knows what possibilities can emerge in the free space of their day. Building their good habits will certainly help them execute on those possibilities with peak performance. It's as simple as that. Lather, rinse, repeat. Everything I have learned about business and life has stemmed from these early lessons. I know establishing habits, and pairing them with your drive, can help you get anywhere you want in life. When building your habits, I'd suggest making them doable, easy, and meaningful towards your life and business goals.

Questions for You

1. What habits support your wellbeing and success?
2. What habits detract from your optimal outcome?
3. What habits do you wish you practiced but currently don't?
4. When will you decide to consciously improve your habits?
5. Where are you most easily able to remain consistent in your habits?

4

Goals

"What you get by achieving your goals is not as important as what you become by achieving your goals."
—Henry David Thoreau

I've told you that I grew up with chaos at home, but I wasn't living in an unsafe environment. West Chester, Pennsylvania, is not exactly the murder capital of the world. Still, I mostly wandered aimlessly through those early years while my home life was being dismantled through my parents' divorce. As life went on, I had many distractions and little structure to counterbalance them. My high school experience did not provide much guidance or clear direction either. I was charting my own path without much of a map.

The first time I visited my high school friend's family beach house, I was stunned. Joe didn't come off as obnoxiously affluent, but his parents did have the resources to take the family on weekend and holiday escapes to their beach house on the Jersey Shore. His family's beach house was nicer than any house I ever lived in. Back then, I thought that only the ultra-rich had second homes and having a beach house was way beyond what I imagined possible.

Spending time at the shore with Joe, I also got the opportunity to spend a little time with a family that shared meals together and enjoyed being with one another. I was being shown this environment, a glimpse into the possibility, and it sparked an inspiration. Maybe, someday, I could have a family and a house like this.

In my late teenage years, as my friends went off to college, I tried my best to stay engaged at the local community college. I found myself in relationships with people who didn't think much beyond the moment, caught up in a "party all the time" environment and inclined to make reckless decisions. This was my social circle, and it wasn't long before trouble caught up with me.

After high school jobs at Burger King and Genuardi's, my immediate post-high school goal was simply *to make money*. I knew I could sell anything, so when I discovered that a local insurance company was hiring, I jumped at the opportunity. At National Liberty, I achieved my goal. I made money selling accidental death and dismemberment insurance and life insurance. I studied to become a professional licensed insurance salesman. I was selling well and hitting the leaderboard which meant I was meeting my goals and making good money. It was the late '80's and I was offered lots of credit cards, too.

No one taught me how to use credit. Even though I was in school and working, I racked up an irresponsible amount of debt. I used my credit to buy my first sports car, a yellow Honda Prelude SI. This car was my "be all and end all." I also indulged by buying sexy leather jackets and lots of clothes for myself. One Christmas, I bought expensive crystal ornaments, unnecessarily, to re-decorate the household Christmas tree. I still keep one of those ornaments for my tree today, a reminder of those early days of erratic spending.

I was buying anything and everything, charging it all. Pretty soon, I'd racked up about $40,000 in debt. I had failing grades for the random courses I was taking at Delaware County Community College and wasn't even following a program that would result in a degree. I was barely holding on at my office job, showing up late, hungover, bleary eyed and smelling like cigarettes. I was not earning enough money to pay the minimum monthly payments on my mounting debt.

I had become a real drag to my mother, who insisted I needed to move out and grow up. I had friends to move in with, but our residence of choice required multiple housemates who were also in the habit of excessive partying. I was living fast and furious. We partied all the time, and the only goals I set were *who I could date next* or *where's the next party?* At this time in my life, I was smoking cigarettes at work, in bed before I went to sleep, when I woke up in the morning, and anytime in between. I constantly reeked of smoke. Talk about the opposite of peak performance. Physically, I thought I was going to die.

The fast and furious had become the reckless and dangerous. My job performance had markedly declined and my relationships were strained. Finally, that new Honda Prelude SI got repossessed. Not having my fancy sports car anymore was pretty embarrassing. I can still recall that sinking feeling of not making payments for so long that eventually the repo man pulled up out front, under the cover of darkness, and drove the car to the impound lot. I was waking up to the truth that my life was starting to fall apart and my reputation was becoming that of a complete loser.

People around me noticed that I was on a decline. At the time, I was fortunate enough to work with a woman named Amy who would remind me that I looked like shit. *"You were out until four in the morning? How can we promote you if you look like this? Take care of yourself."*

There was no intervention or dramatic pep talk that turned me around. The more people told me that I was acting like an idiot, the more I started to hear them and see it in myself. I was starting to become an embarrassment to the community I lived in. Who in my hometown wanted to claim a guy in his early twenties who reeked of cigarettes, couldn't take care of his finances, and prided himself on being at the next party? I was unhealthy, smelly, and wasting my life. I was becoming a form of the chaos that I had grown up wanting to escape.

What did I do to solve my existential issues? I needed to set a goal, make a plan, and take action. I recalibrated my living environment and took a strong look at my habits. Even though I was five figures in debt, I knew it was time for me to get my own apartment, replace my old habits with better ones, and take a look at the people I was choosing to hang around with. I realized I needed to get back to routines like those I'd had when I worked at Genuardi's. It was time to put myself on track to build a better life and develop some new relationships that could help lead me back to a success path. This was my *Eureka!* moment, and I knew it was time to get serious about my future.

I rented my friend Frank's parents' condominium by myself. I restructured my life, got into the habit of working out, doing my laundry, and shopping for groceries on a consistent schedule. Habits continued to drive me forward. I was living within a budget and managing my actions against what I could afford. I also picked up a class at Delaware County Community College and excelled. These changes would start adding up and the outcomes would soon be evident to those around me. My newfound happiness, career goals, and over all well-being were emerging and I liked how it felt and where it could take me. The sky was my new limit. On Sundays, around four or five o'clock, I would wrap up all the weekend's activities and reserve that time for figuratively and literally laying out my clothes for the next day. I started to spend Sunday evenings getting into the right headspace: going to the grocery store, preparing my meals, and living according to the structure that had helped me succeed and work at peak performance just a few years earlier.

Living on my own, I could distance myself from bad influences and surrounded myself with new friends. The gym was a great place to find like minds for the way I wanted to be. My Mom helped me engage with a debt services company who guided me by negotiating my remaining debt through a consumer credit counseling service. I closed *all* my credit cards and got on a monthly payment plan that allowed me to pay down my debt without filing bankruptcy. It was a ten-year plan that ran roughly $400 a month. I could live with that and still cover my rent, food, and utilities. I was fortunate to receive an inheritance and was able to get completely out of debt in roughly four years. I bought another new car and effectively started my money game over. I was about 25 years old.

My coworkers at Verizon started to see how hard I was working, and one day another department manager, Linda, pulled me aside to offer some financial advice:

"Scott, do you know that if you put one percent of your paycheck into our corporate 401(k), you'll have $1,000 in a year? In three years, you'll have $5,000. And in five years, you'll have $20,000. You won't even feel the amount you take home go down significantly. And, the company will match your contribution, so you're giving yourself a raise as well."

At first, I was wary and concerned about saving anything while trying to pay off my debts. But, I listened and ultimately this caring manager was right. Like the Phoenix Rising, my net worth started rising from the ashes of severe debt. Years later, I was able to borrow against my 401(k) savings to buy Katelyn's engagement ring and take a loan as a down payment for my first townhouse. I share this with you, dear reader, because perhaps you, too, can benefit from my corporate manager's advice from thirty years ago.

Start young, save a little, let it compound, and think wisely about how you choose to spend. If your early career has you working for a company with a savings plan and a match, maximize the opportunity.

Around this time, another situation surfaced in my life, one that brought big changes. I was offered the opportunity to work on a special assignment in Virginia Beach. It was time to leave Pennsylvania, and all that was familiar. Going to Virginia opened up the next chapter of my life.

In Virginia Beach, I continued to focus on my plan and I was able to begin fresh, with new coworkers and managers. Sticking to my routine and practicing good habits, I wasn't just checking things off my daily "to-do list." I was building a new lifestyle, networking, and operating at peak performance. The results were astonishing to me.

The Entrepreneur's Path

My years at Verizon were a time of setting numerous goals and I have introduced you to the important people who have been a part of my life and taught me a great deal about setting goals, building relationships, working hard, and practicing good habits.

As the years went on, I added another goal on the financial side of my life. Instead of working for another business' bottom line, I decided to earn a real estate license and started my own company, Worldgate, LLC. By becoming a real estate professional, I could write off certain taxes on the investment properties I owned and benefit from another vehicle for revenue: passive income. I felt my corporate salary had a ceiling, especially since completing a college degree was eluding me. I was learning the potential and freedom that selling and investing in real estate offered me, so I made it one of my short- and long-term goals. *"Work smarter, not harder"* became a personal motto.

With this extra experience and training, I started to understand the foundations of business that I hadn't been able to unearth when I was focused on my corporate position. The path toward self-employment was becoming clearer. As I shared earlier, Worldgate also created the possibility for me to begin consulting.

As I took my first steps as an entrepreneur in real estate and consulting, I realized that setting goals as an entrepreneur looked different from setting goals as an employee. I was at a new learning edge and needed to understand how to set goals, and objectives that would build a plan I could execute.

Entrepreneurship is not always a smooth ride. There are "up weeks" and "down weeks." Business development, managing clients and cash flow, while working as a contractor and not on a salary is all part of an entrepreneur's early life, in the beginning. The "ups" feel magical, and the "downs" feel like your company is going to implode at any minute. Over the years I have learned that setting goals, managing priorities, and sticking to good habits helps reduce anxiety. Some weeks are slow, and others are so packed I don't have five minutes to myself. I have established a habit of evaluating my happiness, my pursuits, and all of the goals I have set for myself regularly. When I need to reassess, I reassess. When I need to reprioritize, I reprioritize.

I have experience building and following through with the priorities in my own life: physical fitness, relationships, and money. As I've identified those priorities, I've planted the seeds and waited to see which start budding. Entrepreneurs have the power to take full control of the seeds they're planting, how much time they tend to them, and how high they want to grow the results that sprout from their work. That's the beauty of entrepreneurship. You set your own goals. It comes at the expense of not knowing exactly which trees are going to bear fruit and which aren't going to make it past being a seedling, but that's OK with me. After years in corporate, my budding entrepreneurial goals focused on being in a place where I could grow my own forest.

And in my forties, I realized my vision, the inspiration that came from going to Joe's family beach house all those years ago. In 2015, Katelyn and I purchased our family beach house, on the Delaware Shore. It's a place where our family of five goes often. We get up in the mornings, have breakfast together, and head to the beach. We enjoy our family time together and I celebrate accomplishing that goal, and remember the seeds planted decades earlier.

Every checkpoint on your journey continues to be an opportunity to assess your goals, adjust them, and make new ones. This is possible every day, week, or year. If you don't like the path you are walking down today, create a goal and find a new path. Paired with focusing on your daily habits, you have the power to go anywhere you want in life.

The Basics of Setting Goals

Why should we set goals in the first place? They propel us forward. Goals transform insurmountable mountains into walkable hills. Without them, we run the risk of wandering aimlessly through life and never reaching the peak of what we can do.

"I want to be financially independent" and "I want to get married within the year" are two very different goals that fit into different categories. I place goals into one of three categories:

1. **Time goals:** completing a cooking recipe in under an hour or having a six-figure job by the end of the year.
2. **Focus goals:** reading a book chapter without becoming distracted or getting up every day and sticking to the same routine.
3. **Topic-based goals:** broader personal goals, professional goals, or financial goals.

Once you're ready to set your goals, you need to deliberate carefully. Write the goals down and decide on the objectives that will bring you toward completing your goals. Goals are *future-oriented*; unto themselves, they don't include actual steps toward accomplishing them. Objectives, on the other hand, are explicit, incremental achievements that are steps toward your goal. They are typically measurable and are associated with a timeline.

Your goal might be to learn how to code well enough to attend a hackathon. An associated objective that helps you achieve that goal might be downloading the Hopscotch app and completing one activity a day.

As you make progress, be sure to celebrate your successes. Just because you are creating structure by setting goals doesn't mean you have to be a drag to complete them. Keep the journey fun.

Everything going on in my life—from writing this book to getting married, having a family, owning real estate, to leadership coaching and serving as chief customer officer of my consulting firm—came from setting goals for myself. But it's not like I set out to write a book thirty years ago or ever thought that I'd become a leadership coach one day. On my journey, I looked out the window. I've always explored the next thing to add to my portfolio, career, or life. I wish I could live forever because I want to keep trying new things, setting new goals, and following new paths from now until eternity!

Just because you set a goal doesn't mean you have to follow it down one path for the rest of your life either. It's my observation that successful people dabble in many different things. All of the people that I emulate or find interesting know this and live this way. They aren't boxed into one profession. Like me, they are writing books, taking courses, and opening varying businesses. They are looking for the next goal to set. Really successful people are open to changing, adjusting, and setting new goals as the emerging path becomes more apparent.

Not all of these paths lead to money, but they can. I believe that money doesn't always equal happiness. Money can help you do a lot of things in your life, it's true. But, keeping a laser focus on making money isn't going to produce the success you think it will. On the flip side, multiple focuses and goals provide multiple opportunities to make money and build wealth. These focuses may fulfill you in other ways too. The only way you'll find out is by exploring these paths and setting goals.

Make sure you establish goals that you genuinely want to achieve, rather than create goals that you feel like you *have* to reach or reach for *others*. You don't have to make a certain salary just because your neighbors do. You don't have to get married because all of your friends are getting married, or your mother is griping that you're still single. You get to set your own goals.

Once you've determined what your goals are, create a one-year plan, a six-month plan, and a one-month plan. Then, create a daily to-do list of objectives that will incrementally bring you closer to your goals. Maintain your passion for achieving your goals by reviewing and updating your to-do list regularly. Goals aren't tattoos, and you can always modify your long-term plans to reflect your changing priorities and the vagaries of life. Remember: Keep your goals manageable, measurable, and meaningful.

If you're unsure how to start, the SMART strategy can be helpful (**s**pecific, **m**easurable, **a**chievable, **r**ealistic, and **t**ime-bound). Think of a SMART goal as a series of objectives that make the goal doable:

- **Specific: Clear and well-defined.** A specific goal has a much greater chance of being accomplished than a general one. Ask yourself, with respect to your specific goal: Who is involved? What do you want to accomplish? What is the timeframe? What will be the requirements and constraints? What are your reasons for pursuing the goal? What will the benefits of achieving it be?

- **Measurable: Quantifiable.** Establish concrete criteria for measuring progress toward the attainment of each goal that you set. When you measure your progress, you stay on track, reach your target dates, and experience the exhilaration of achievement that spurs you to continue on.

- **Achievable: Make sure the goals can actually be accomplished.** When you identify goals that are most important to you, you need to figure out ways to attain them. You should develop the attitudes, abilities, skills, and financial requirements necessary to reach your goals.

- **Realistic: A goal must be something that you are both willing and able to work towards.** You are the only person who can decide just how 'high' your goal should be.

- **Time-bound: Without a timeline, you are far more likely to 'fall off the wagon.'** Without a timeline, there is no sense of urgency.

Without explicit goals, it can be very easy to deceive ourselves into thinking we're on the right track. No matter where you are in life, decide *now* what you want, and how you can take steps on the path towards that goal. You might not achieve your goal in a day, or a month, or even a year. But the first step is the most important, and *that* is attainable today.

<u>Questions for You</u>

1. Why is setting goals important *to you*?
2. What are your goals in the short-term, medium-term, long-term?
3. Who encourages and supports you in reaching your goals?
4. What goal have you achieved that gave you greatest satisfaction?
5. What goals have you set that no longer serve you?

5
Mentor...Advisor... Coach

"Coaching is unlocking a person's potential to maximize their own performance."
—John Whitmore

No one launches and builds a successful company alone. Even if you are a 'solopreneur,' you'll find that you need to engage others who'll bring their subject matter expertise—legal, financial, organizational guidance, branding, marketing, products and services support, and more. It begins with *you* and your vision, ideas, and ambition that can drive you to set a goal to create something. In my experience, I have come to understand that it takes a *collective* to build a successful company.

As a realtor, I became an independent contractor, and this was quite different from my time working in corporate as an employee. Gone were the regular hours, salary, and directives from managers. I was responsible for managing my time and had to cover *all* my expenses. Working on a commission basis created *opportunities* for unlimited financial return on my efforts. It also meant that I had significant money—and a good amount of time—invested on the front-side, before I ever made any commissions. These included my real estate course, licensing test and fees, business cards, and signage. I was ready to take the risk because the rewards held greater potential.

Katelyn and I started Worldgate LLC as a company to hold my work as a realtor, as well as our investment properties, while limiting our liabilities and managing our tax obligations. I was already well aware of the value of relationships, and I continued to turn to them. I knew I needed to reach out to others who had more experience. There is a lot to learn when you are starting out. Getting good advice when you are forming your own business—from an attorney, accountant, or the Small Business Administration—is essential when you launch a business.

The relationships I had built over my years at Verizon and the guidance offered to me by several folks continued to serve me well as I transitioned. Those early managers offered me insights into organizational dynamics and helped me understand the company culture. They offered suggestions about what I needed to learn and skills I needed to develop, so I could progress. These were my mentors, and they were giving me the gifts of their time and experiences. As they introduced me to people in *their* networks, I broadened my interactions and this helped me gain visibility as an "up and comer," contributing to my advancement opportunities. As a mentee, I appreciated the time they spent with me. I listened to their feedback, and I followed their guidance. I also thanked them for their generosity frequently.

Relationships are the cornerstone to my "getting here." When I moved into real estate, I found a mentor, for the same reasons that I wanted that support in my previous profession. I was stepping into a new "business" and there was much I didn't know, as well as people I needed to meet. Jennifer opened up so many avenues and connections. She also taught me process-driven ways of doing the work that helped me find success sooner and with less stress. I want to impress upon you the importance of being mentored and being an engaged mentee, as you are on your path. I continue to have mentors in various areas of my life, it's not just beneficial in the early years.

***

I first met Gretchen when I was selling real estate. She and her husband Paul owned a condo in Arlington that they had been trying to sell for six months. I was an ambitious agent with Keller Williams and every time I showed her condo, I'd leave my business card. And one afternoon, she reached out.

"You've been showing our property a lot," she said. *"I'm struggling to sell this place and the listing is coming up. I would like to talk with you about listing it."* After our first lively conversation, I was hired. I'd had that somatic response when we met, as Gretchen and I had many

things in common, including having real estate experience. The real estate market was softening, so I had my work cut out for me to get her unit sold. The day she called to talk with me about pulling the listing so she could rent, rather than sell, I brought in a buyer who was willing to sign on the dotted line. The transaction was a sign to both of us that destiny was on our side. After the closing, we stayed in touch.

As the Recession of 2008 impacted the housing market, I was fortunate that consulting opportunities increased and I could bring my IT consulting skills forward. As the client work increased, I found myself leading Worldgate in a broader direction—still holding my real estate role—as well as expanding into IT implementation and staffing for the K-12 educational market. By 2010, I'd hired two employees to manage the implementation and operational needs of our growing business.

***

Gretchen and I met up for coffee at Starbucks that spring. She and I had stayed in touch over the years. She'd refer potential clients to me, we found we had a lot to talk about and enjoyed one another's company. When I first met Gretchen in 2007, she was working as an organizational consultant and executive coach. She had spent years as a teacher/trainer and facilitator, built her own entrepreneurial and professional service practices, and worked in partnership with her former spouse. It was good to sit down together and as she listened to me, I shared about the growth we were experiencing and Worldgate's opportunities to expand its consulting services. I also shared that we were in a dynamic time with the business and our family, with significant competing demands on my time and attention as Katelyn and I were growing the company.

What happened in that early conversation was my introduction to the potency of being in a coaching relationship. Gretchen asked me questions that invited me to identify the issues I was needing to address and the impact they were having on me, personally and professionally. She asked questions and *listened,* without offering advice or interruption. In that space we shared, I heard myself thinking out loud, and as the hour passed, she reflected back what she'd noticed and invited me to share what *I thought* would help me move forward.

Gretchen and I continued to talk about what was emerging for Worldgate and in autumn of that year she and her husband Paul—both process consultants and executive coaches—brought their expertise for integrating people, process, and technology to guide us in our formative years at Worldgate. Over several months, they facilitated and advised Katelyn and me as we articulated our Vision, Mission, Values, and Purpose. They were there in the early years, as we built a strategy that helped us target our marketing, build our business processes, and hire additional staff. Twelve years in, we continue to draw upon their expertise as strategic advisors who present us with solutions and assist us with process improvements, as well as coaches who ask the questions and hold space for what rises from within. That synchronistic relationship I sparked with Gretchen, selling her condo, evolved into years of us working together.

At Worldgate, we still have those graphic illustrations from that early in-depth process. Looking at them twelve years in, I see our foundation is still strong and the original intentions continue to guide our culture and company. There have been many twists and turns along the way, and as a leader, I have needed to draw upon the expertise of Gretchen and Paul—as well as many other professional resources—to build our success. Mentors, advisors, and coaches have contributed so much to my learning and leadership.

For me, what's been important about being in an ongoing coaching relationship is that it allows me to continually assess what I want as I am pursuing my goals, honoring my values, and understanding the impact upon myself, my family, and our company. Building a multi-million-dollar company often requires that you make sacrifices, and it is essential to continue paying attention to what *really* matters to you, at the very core. Because Katelyn and I have been intentional about why we wanted to start Worldgate, we prioritize how we spend our time, taking care to focus on our family while managing the competing demands on our time and energy needed to run our thriving business.

***

I'd been coaching with Gretchen for a number of years and over time, the depth of our conversations and my development as a leader had progressed. Learning more about myself through assessments and team development work that we've done at Worldgate—as well as receiving feedback from my employees on our company culture and my leadership—gave me insights and I found myself wanting to learn more.

In 2017, she encouraged me to enroll in a coaching certification program at George Mason University. Though skeptical at first, I took a long look at their Leadership Coaching for Organizational Wellbeing program. Soon, I found myself immersed in a rigorous six-month executive cohort, learning from some of the top executive coaches in the DC area. After months of study and coaching practice, I became ACC-certified by the International Coaching Federation ACC-level coaching.

Getting Results

After I completed my certification, I began coaching. One of my first clients, Rob, was my eldest son's basketball coach. I held our coaching sessions in my living room. He and I were in different places in our lives; my new client was still building on his emerging career. He would look around my house and ask me, *"How did you get here?"*

He wanted to set goals that aligned with where I was, both personally and financially. But he didn't just want to make more money; he also wanted to be in an industry that challenged him. He was working as a part-time recruiter and teaching basketball. He had a small basketball camp that brings in a little bit of money, but he was not satisfied with that as a career play and wanted more.

Questions like: *"What are you doing right now to make money?" "What's your idea of success?"* and *"What interests do you have?"* guided our conversation to the point where he shared that he was ultimately interested in real estate.

In time, our coaching led to mentoring, and I shared my experiences and asked him again what path he would like to take to achieve his idea of success. I knew firsthand how the investments you make in real estate don't have a return until usually months later. So I made him an offer. I told him I would help subsidize his real estate launch costs and coach him as he studied. There was one condition: He wasn't allowed to quit his recruiting job and dive headfirst into real estate without setting goals and putting a plan together. Success, first and foremost, meant being able to put food on his table.

We shook hands, and a few months later he passed his licensing exam. Today, Rob is a successful real estate agent at the Keller Williams Office where I also hang my license. He is putting in the work to build his network and lift his practice. I will always make time to support and coach him as his career and life progresses.

I meet coaching clients the same way that I met some of the most influential people in my life. They are often the everyday people I find myself interacting with. A few years ago, I was surprised when a personal trainer at my gym offered me a free personal training session one afternoon during my work out. Ron had seen my efforts at the gym over some time and thought I could use some guidance with my workout routine. As we got to talking, he admitted that being a personal trainer wasn't putting him on the path that he had envisioned for himself. He was doing the work well, but he expressed concern that it wasn't making him happy.

At that moment, I saw an opportunity and asked him if I could help. Ron was able to strike up a conversation with me in a way that only a good salesman can. What's more, we knew a few things about each other because we both stuck to our habit of going to the gym regularly. After a preliminary conversation I thought he might benefit more from some strategic advice. I had no doubts about telling him that pursuing other opportunities could be more satisfying, perhaps in sales. He wasn't going to make the salary he wanted in the career path he was on, but he could exceed it with ease by picking up the phone and having conversations just like the one he struck with me.

In the weeks ahead, I learned that this wasn't advice he had ever heard before. In fact, no one in his peer group had bothered to give him any advice. He surrounded himself with people who saw him as nothing more than a fitness enthusiast. They didn't see how his ability to forge relationships, stick to habits, and use exceptional communication skills could be applied to another career. We engaged in several coaching sessions at my office and as I watched him embracing change and making the effort to build another career path, it was very extremely rewarding.

Today, I see Ron at the gym and in my neighborhood. He offered me condolences for the loss of my brother and gave me an update on his life. Since we've known each other, he's transitioned to leading a sales team, elevated his career, and found the happiness that he thought was out of reach when he was working at the gym. Recently, he sent me a text offering thanks:

"Hey, Scott, just wanted to let you know, today's my one-year anniversary. As I was reflecting this morning on the past year of my career, you took center stage in my thoughts. I want to let you know I'm crushing it here.

"I've just been elevated to senior sales development rep. I'm already looking ahead to what my next move is. Thank you for helping me get to where I am. Thank you for seeing something in the personal trainer who handed out protein shake samples that he didn't see in himself.

"Your guidance has been the main catalyst for getting myself into a position that I'm happy with. Your coaching

has given me subtle confidence in every one of my interactions with colleagues and peers.

"My first day here, I took your advice and offered my supervisor a breath mint. And now I consider him my most valuable professional connection. To sum it up, thank you for everything, I hope we reconnect soon, and I hope you're helping others the way you've helped me."

I believe we all need to establish goals and create plans to accomplish what we seek. We all need to build stronger habits. We also benefit when there is someone we can trust, be honest with, and who is willing to hold us accountable. Imagine the text you might send to your coach one day, in appreciation for their support in catalyzing your success. If you are willing to make the commitment, before you know it, people will be asking *you, "How did you get here?"*

***

As leadership and performance coaching continues to grow in visibility, I am often asked about the difference between coaching, therapy, and consulting.

Coaching is about personal inquiry and self-discovery. A coach will ask open-ended questions rather than give you answers. They focus on helping you discover your strengths, weaknesses, personality type, and can help you think about how you are engaging as a leader. A coach may notice patterns and trends in the answers the client gives, but their first priority is not to offer solutions. The coach's goal is to help facilitate the client's identified purpose for the session.

Therapy is different from Coaching. Counselors, Psychologists, and Psychiatrists can help you in important ways when your needs require. They are trained to focus on earlier life experiences in a way that helps you understand why your relationships, childhood experiences, patterns, and behaviors may be affecting certain situations in your life.

Strategic Advisors are consultants. When you hire an advisor, you are paying for their experience, so expect to be told what to do. You're engaging someone who can assess the situation you present and can work within the organization to identify issues unseen. They will answer your questions and make recommendations to solve the issues you are dealing with.

***

When I engage in a coaching conversation, I intend to create a space where I am able to meet the client where they are and offer an environment in which I can listen deeply to what is most important to the person across from me—be it in the room, on the phone, or on Zoom. The questions I ask are almost always open-ended. You can't answer, "What do you expect from today?" with a "yes" or a "no." When you are in a coaching session, you should feel stimulated to think, dig, and pull out more elaborate answers than you are accustomed to. This will help direct the coach to the next question and guide you to your next steps, bringing forth those *a-ha* moments.

Coaches often start conversations with questions like:

- What do you want to explore?
- What do you want to walk away with?
- What is important to you?
- How will we know we're successful?

As the coaching session closes, coaches may ask questions like:

- What's the most meaningful takeaway from this session?
- What do you want to do with this?
- What support do you have, and what are your obstacles?
- How will you hold yourself accountable?
- How did we do? Did you get what you needed?

These can be very potent questions to ask someone. When you can answer these questions and listen to your internal guidance, you may find the path is opening wide and all you have to do is start walking. Having a trusted thought partner to share the journey is the value of working with a coach.

Twelve years into our shared time, I have had the benefit of learning and growing through many life events with Gretchen as a coach, mentor, advisor, and friend. She is a 'story-catcher' who will reflect her own life experiences if there is something that might offer guidance to me. When my brother Dan died and the world shifted on its axis, she offered me great support and shared the wisdom gained through the untimely death of her own brother. She and Paul have been there for me at that difficult time and through the transition that followed. As Worldgate continues to offer our clients leadership and team development and coaching, my work with Gretchen continues.

Questions for You

1. Who are the mentors you have or had in your life?
2. What experiences have you had working with a coach? With an advisor?
3. How could working with a coach help you achieve your goals?
4. Who is someone you can look to for coaching?
5. How could you incorporate coaching into your path towards success?

6

Communication

Communication is important to all our relationships. As an extroverted person, I have come to understand my way of talking with people can be very high-energy. I tend to have a lot to say and have not always listened as well as I might. Over time, I have come to understand my need to "talk to think" and it's definitely been one of the benefits of working with a coach. As I have developed my awareness of my communication *"style,"* I have also learned about *others'* style of communication. Those who are more introverted prefer to listen, may need time to process their thinking, and then, offer their response. Yes, I've mowed down many an introvert in my day and that means I've lost opportunities to slow myself down enough to hear their ideas and get their input. As a leader, working with my team, the benefits of coach training have been learning and understanding *myself* better so I can create more inclusive and engaging opportunities for my employees and coaching clients.

When I was a newly-licensed agent with Keller Williams, I remember taking the DiSC® assessment. The company used DiSC® to help us build stronger and more effective working relationships. This popular assessment helps raise self-awareness, including what motivates or stresses you out, how you might respond to conflict, and how you solve problems. It also helps you communicate with team members, as each of us has our own "working style." It also helped me become more effective as a salesperson, because I learned how to adapt my style to my client's styles.

DiSC® is an acronym that stands for the four main personality profiles described in the DiSC® model: (D)ominance, (i)nfluence, (S)teadiness, and (C)onscientiousness.

People with D personalities *tend to be confident and place an emphasis on accomplishing bottom-line results.*

People with i personalities *tend to be more open and place an emphasis on relationships and influencing or persuading others.*

People with S personalities *tend to be dependable and place the emphasis on cooperation and sincerity.*

People with C personalities *tend to place the emphasis on quality, accuracy, expertise, and competency.*

My results were insightful. I am a clear 'D' dominant and everything I read about being *driven* and *result-oriented* rang true. Learning more about my Driver-style was helpful and I felt "seen" reading my results. In those early years, I was also impatient with others who did not seem to appreciate my energetic "D." Learning more about other "styles" and how I can *"meet people where they are"* took on additional meaning. Over the years, I have come to value what can be accomplished by leveraging the diversity of styles on my team. Yes, I am still very much a "D," but I am glad we use DiSC® at Worldgate with our managers, employees, and our clients so I have insights into how to adapt my style and strengthen our working relationships.

Worldgate has built its success over these years because of the relationships we have cultivated with our clients, our employees, and in our community. Katelyn and I both value relationships and that foundation was set for Worldgate LLC back in 2010 when we crafted our Vision and Mission. Our professional development as leaders and employers is our investment in building our own capacity—and inviting our people to develop theirs—so we all communicate effectively, giving and receiving feedback, resolving conflicts in a timely manner, and keeping our commitments to values we stand upon and the culture we want to uphold.

The Myers Briggs Type Indicator® (MBTI®), CliftonStrengths, and DiSC® are core assessments that we utilize to train our people and help our managers work with greater effectiveness and engagement with their teams. I believe our excellent retention rate of employees and clients is because of our relational sales ethos and ongoing initiatives that enhance self-awareness and improve communication skills.

As a leader who is invested in coaching my people rather than telling them what to do, I have had the opportunity to draw upon my training. Mind you, I am still a work in progress, and I am sharing this story to reflect my discovery.

I used a coaching approach recently when working with a Worldgate employee. A senior manager has been described as "difficult" or "arrogant"; this person tended to speak to people in a demeaning way. Their somewhat pessimistic attitude was turning a lot of people off during meetings and the client was becoming frustrated with the negativity this manager was bringing to project meetings.

I have known this experienced manager to be an excellent analyst, trustworthy, and honest. They wanted to be direct with the client, but it was coming across as impatient and brusque. What was being conveyed didn't align with the message that they *thought* they were communicating. I was surprised that when I brought the client's feedback to their attention, this manager did not recognize the other people's perceptions of them. I arranged for a Leadership Circle Profile—a 360 survey—to solicit feedback from numerous evaluators, including the manager's direct reports, peers, clients, and myself, as their boss. Sharing the results and reading through the comments, the manager and I gained access to important information. They were highly regarded and worked well with their direct reports. Their challenges were in managing "up," meaning how they interacted with leaders above them in the organization. This impacted their effectiveness with their clients, but also other senior leaders and partners.

Rather than just saying, *"Change your attitude. Go read a book on how to be nicer. Get some training because everyone thinks you're arrogant,"* we took a deeper look and gathered information that reflected back to the manager the ways they were perceived. This individual was open to joining me in coaching conversations and I brought questions and compassion to our interactions. In time, they shared their frustrations with the role they were holding, and we came to discover—through their DiSC® profile and their Strengths—it was better to pivot them from direct, high-touch client-facing responsibilities into a more productive and aligned role within the organization.

Compassion and Communication

Rasmus Hougard, CEO of the Potential Project, makes these distinctions between *empathy* and *compassion* in leadership:

"Compassion starts with empathy and then turns outward, with an intent to help. With compassion, leaders make the conscious choice to turn emotion into

action. And in doing so, compassionate leaders are perceived as stronger and more competent, able to make decisions and get things done. And, compassion in an organization triggers other positive outcomes: improved collaboration, trust, and team loyalty."

In order to meet your people where they are, have compassion for where they might be. And by "your people," I'm talking about our clients too. Keeping compassion in mind helps me to communicate with more impact.

***

Recently, I was on a call with a client. I knew from previous conversations and working with my team that there would be many personalities contributing to this call and we were going to be discussing the renewal of our contracts. I was tasked with juggling several different styles and my intention was to keep my expectations open and hear what they had to say.

"How are you doing today?"

"What are you thinking about the direction of the project?"

"What are we doing that is working well for you?"

"What could we do to make things better?"

"What are your goals for this particular project? Talk to me about what you want."

I needed to gauge where everyone was and listen to understand how we were meeting their needs, and where we weren't. I needed to ask open-ended questions and *listen* for what challenges they were trying to solve and timelines they needed to meet. Rather than jumping in and telling them what they needed, I was able to draw from that place of compassion to feel their mood and emotion. I wanted to support their cause, and I made that known.

By the time the call ended, I'd added *more* services to our contract. Our Worldgate controller was on the call and I appreciated her feedback on how I had led and communicated effectively by asking the questions I did. Instead of selling, I *inquired*, I *offered*, I *partnered*. This is how I gauge effective communication.

When I receive a complaint about an employee or a client, I resist the temptation to tell the complainer, *"Well, just go fix it."* Instead, I'll ask questions:

"Why do you think that call went poorly?"

"How are you feeling about it?"

"Help me understand how you think it could have gone differently?"

These questions can help the person think through what the issues are and how they can handle things. Rather than "telling" someone how to do it, ask questions, then listen. Reflect back. This is how you can help another to find their way, allowing compassion to rise.

The Basics of Our Communication

Care and compassion are fundamental to me, in and out of the office. They lay a foundation for communication that fits the criteria of the seven C's that we at Worldgate work to instill in all our communications. We promote communication that is *Clear, Concise, Concrete, Correct, Coherent, Complete,* and *Courteous.* These are the overarching goals of every email that we send, every phone call we make, and every meeting we conduct.

Reaching our communication goals requires nine skills. Practicing and building on these skills will make you a better communicator; I promise you that. These skills are:

1. Nonverbal communication
2. Active listening
3. Asking questions
4. Being clear and succinct
5. Clarifying and summarizing
6. Being empathetic
7. Providing feedback
8. Developing trust and rapport
9. Being present

Nonverbal Communication

I'm often deliberate in my body language. I'm always very purposeful in the way I lean in and the way I position myself relative to the other person in any conversation. Small changes in one's nonverbal cues have a big impact on how any message is being conveyed. Fifty-five percent of communication is done through *body language*, thirty-eight percent is through *tone of voice*, and only seven percent is through *what is actually said*. Keep this in mind when you seek to be more impactful. Your body language "speaks" as does someone else's body language, so pay attention. Your tone of voice and your pace of speech matter, too.

I believe that the positive professional interactions I experience with most people are the results of my open body language and style of engagement. Saying to someone, *"I'm interested in what you have to say"* is not as powerful as facing your body *toward* them, nodding your head, and keeping your hands folded (as opposed to holding your arms crossed tightly by your body). People sometimes like to be touched as well, but we need to be mindful of touch in the workplace. I'm intentional about how and when I use touch to reassure someone or to grab their attention. How can someone believe that you're fully focused when you look like you're going to hop out of your seat? Even if a person doesn't consciously think about where your feet are pointed or how your arms are positioned, they feel your energy. That's why I align my body's position as well.

Actively Listening

Of course, body language isn't all that matters. You have to back up your nonverbal communication by actively listening. Continue to redirect your focus from what is going on in your own mind and instead focus on the needs of the person speaking to you.

All of the nine communication skills I've named and engaging with empathy opens you to listen to the other person with the intention to understand what they are feeling, thinking, and experiencing. When I am actively listening, I am quiet, attentive, and opening my mind to truly hear what the other person is saying, rather than formulating my response. When I speak, it is to reflect back to the speaker what I have heard them say. This gives them an opportunity to correct misinformation or expand on their story. Again, when actively listening, I am the receiver, rather than the responder. Asking open-ended questions in order to better understand, without steering the conversation away from the speaker's intention, can take the conversation further, allowing for context and greater clarity. Summarize what you have heard.

Wait patiently until that message comes across and is confirmed before you can disclose your opinion. There are a few ways that you might build trust when it's your turn to offer your response or feedback to the message that has been communicated. You can provide brief verbal affirmations or demonstrate sympathetic responses through verbal and nonverbal communication to show that you understand.

You aren't going to find the right solution until you have received a clear message from the person on the other end of the conversation. Putting assumptions aside and using active listening is the only way to ensure that you receive that message.

Asking Questions

I believe in asking open-ended *how, when,* and *what* questions when communicating with someone. You're going to get informative answers by asking someone, "What is your idea of success?" rather than, "Are you successful?" Specific open-ended questions often start with "when," "where," "who," "which," "how much," and "how many." Avoid close-ended questions that can begin with "did," "do," "would," "will," "should," "could," "have," "must," "is," and "are."

Being Clear and Succinct

The flood of information we all endure daily can be overwhelming. Texts and emails require effective communication skills because we miss the body language and may misconstrue the "tone." Using virtual tools to meet like Zoom and Teams are now part of our workplace and increase our need to attend to our "presence," pay attention to our body language, and focus on how we contribute to the conversation through voice and chat. It can be helpful to plan your communication before actually engaging so your message comes across clearly and succinctly. To do so, you'll need to understand your objectives and your audience and work to speak *precisely* and *concisely*.

Keep in mind that you are the source of the message that you want to share. To get that message to the receiver, you have to want to encode that message effectively for the decoder. Encoding is the process of creating a clear, well-crafted message. When encoding a message, be sure to know what you want to say, decide exactly how to say it, consider the recipient's perspective, choose words that leave no room for miscommunication, and monitor your content and tone.

All of this may be done slightly differently when you consider *how* you are sharing a message. The way you write a message may not directly translate to how you'd speak that message. There are different rules for different forms of communication. When deciding between channels, such as email, text, face-to-face, or voice message, consider the sensitivity of the subject, audience, time constraints, and relative importance of feedback.

Written Communication

Your ability to write effective professional communications, distinct from the casual style of personal texting, include a proper salutation and a coherent and concise message that is written in complete sentences with punctuation. Business emails should include a signature with your name, email, and telephone number, at the very least. Do the necessary work to create concise communications, making sure your message addresses the issue(s) and any offers or requests you want to make. Re-read and spell check the message before hitting SEND. In order to convey your message most effectively, you must consider and choose the right channel of communication: text, email, or direct message.

Text messaging has become prevalent in the workplace. Although it tends to be a casual medium, it is always a good idea to maintain professional etiquette while texting colleagues. Think of texting as a conversation. It has been my experience to avoid EVER texting anything confidential, private, or potentially embarrassing.

If you decide an email is the right approach, keep these guidelines in mind:

- Always have a clear subject line and talk about only one subject per email.
- Begin your message with a salutation.
- Don't assume that the recipient knows what you are talking about.
- Make sure you have a signature that includes you name and contact information.
- Don't default to "Reply All," and only send replies to people who need to read the email.

Clarifying and Summarizing

When in a communication with someone, whether in person or through written form, it serves you to clarify the sender's information and requests through questions. Then, summarize what you have heard so you can proceed with clarity. Don't you feel more comfortable when a person repeats back your food order or your phone number? Give people that comfort, whether you're discussing numbers or higher-level concepts. Be sure to address any requests of you directly.

Being Empathetic and Compassionate

I cannot reiterate enough how important empathy and compassion are to communication. These are often called "soft skills," but I argue that they are both essential and *leadership skills* to effective communication. Learn the difference between the two. Rasmus Hougard, who described the distinction between empathy and compassion that we discussed earlier, added more differences between the two, which we all need to consider:

"Empathy is considered the reflexive and automatic part of our psychology which originates in the emotion centers of the brain. Empathetic feelings, thoughts, and decisions are generated mostly on an unconscious level, which means we are less aware and less intentional about those decisions.

"Compassion is considered the reflective and deliberate part of our psychology which originates in the cognitive

centers of the brain. Compassionate feelings, thoughts, and decisions pass through filters of consciousness, which means we can deliberate, reflect, and improve on the decisions."

I have found, when communicating with others, that my increasing awareness of how I *feel* guides the actions I take and when this is grounded in compassion, I am bringing my best.

Providing Feedback

Giving and receiving feedback is essential, and we all react or respond to feedback in different ways. The assessments that I spoke of earlier offer insights into people's different "styles" of communication. There is so much value in having the knowledge and awareness of my own personal "style," and understanding my employees' "styles" when it comes to communicating in a pro-active—rather than reactive—way. Many people have a fear and aversion to feedback, often because of experiences from earlier in life.

I find approaching with empathy is the key to providing feedback that reduces the risk of coming across as confrontational. When I have empathy for the person across the table, I seek to prevent a problem and reduce the distance between us.

I'm a non-confrontational guy. There are times when I want to avoid awkward conversations or take the easy way out. Unfortunately, the easy way out often leads to miscommunication and any problem typically lingers on much longer than necessary, and it can actually expand beyond the original scope. Problems don't get solved that way. People stay stagnant. You have to do the work if you want to see the results.

As a leader, I want to share that communicating-in-conflict is a leadership skill that I continue to work on *daily*. I want to be more effective in accomplishing the best outcomes for my relationships and for our business. I have found that I need to bring greater clarity and conciseness to the conversation when giving feedback. Finding the appropriate time and place, entering the conversation with the intention to create a positive outcome, and offering timely and specific feedback—while listening to clarify and comprehend—are all good practices.

Our culture at Worldgate is based on having a Learners' Mindset, and I work to keep our culture in mind at all times. We seek to hire people who demonstrate they are open to learning and, as a company, Katelyn and I are committed to training and supporting our employees to develop their communications skills. This benefits our internal and client-focused interactions as well as our personal lives, because we know that relationships are built and maintained by the quality of communications shared.

Questions for You

1. Who in your life communicates well?
2. What do you see are your strengths and weaknesses in communicating?
3. How do you feel about giving or receiving feedback?
4. What could you do in order to listen more?
5. How would building better communication skills help you in achieving your goals?

7
Mindset & Self-Care

"When you go from a fixed mindset to a growth mindset, a new world of possibilities opens up."
—Keller Williams Realty

During the early years of my career, I learned skills and built habits that have helped me progress toward success. Developing healthy habits and a self-care routine has been essential so that I am able to show up mentally and physically prepared. As a teenager, I did not know about good nutrition, and no one showed me how to lift weights until I was eighteen. But once I started going to the gym and eating healthy foods, I began to feel better and stronger. I find that my body does better without heavy carbohydrates, sugar, and alcohol. Not too much caffeine, keeping myself well-hydrated with water throughout the day, and eating foods that fuel a balanced mood and give me reserves I need to live the active life I do has been a process of self-discovery.

I have a natural curiosity and I have been willing to listen and learn from others. Feedback has been my friend, and I have come to understand that my Growth Mindset has been significant to my success.

In 1988, Dr. Carol S. Dweck first presented her research-based model to show the impact of mindsets. She showed how a person's mindset sets the stage for either performance goals or learning goals. It's all about our internal perspectives and how we make meaning. And Mindset is foundational to our learning and culture at Worldgate.

Someone who operates from a Fixed Mindset is more focused on *performing well* so they look good and smart. When confronted with obstacles, they tend to give up and don't see that making an effort is worthwhile. They often ignore criticism and feel threatened by the success of others. Fixed Mindset *sees self and others as possessing a set amount of cognitive and physical ability; i.e., "I'm not smart enough to do this."*

Someone operating from a Growth Mindset is interested *in learning*. They are more willing to embrace challenges, they'll persevere in the face of setbacks, put in the effort to overcome obstacles, and take criticism as information to help them do better. They are also inspired by the success of others. Growth Mindset *sees self and others as being constant learners and abilities evolving and growing; i.e., "I'm not smart enough to do this, YET."*

A Growth Mindset holds potential, and *intelligence* and *abilities can be developed through effort, persistence, trying different strategies, and learning from mistakes.* Thirty years in, I know that having a Growth Mindset continues to propel me forward.

Self-Care

Training in the gym, preparing for a triathlon, or working with my leadership coach all contribute to me building my capacity to show up as the leader, partner, and father I want to be. Managing one's energy and practicing good self-care are also essential to optimal performance. When people ask, "How did you get here?" I would be remiss to not mention the results I've achieved from ritual self-care practices and emotional fitness. I've learned to choose positivity, even when faced with unforeseen obstacles. I can choose how I respond to what life throws my way, but it has taken me years to develop my practices that help me stay present in the face of disruptions.

Running, lifting weights, biking—you might not name these activities as self-care—but having daily, active exercise is essential for my body and clears my mind. I get away from the technology that bombards me and requires a response. Having time to let my mind wander, noticing my pace, my breathing, and allowing intuition to offer me guidance are benefits I have found in exercise.

A few years ago, I started booking massages. I leave the masseuse feeling more open than I ever had before. Stress and toxins that had been building up in my body just flowed out of my pores. The benefit of having regular massage is that my body responds by relaxing deeply and opening areas of held experiences that can create chronic discomfort. After a massage, I am ready to go further… one more mile on the bike, one more brainstorming session at work, etc. Before the COVID pandemic, my clients knew that there was no reaching me at 4:00 p.m. on Fridays—I was at my massage. I know it's a privilege to be able to go to a spa. The money I spend on massages is like the money I'm spending on a coach: I see it as an investment in myself.

I have also found that Mindfulness exercises have been helpful in quieting my very busy mind. Settling comfortably in a chair, I gently close my eyes and inhale deeply, counting to four, holding my breath, for a count of four, then a slow exhale, again counting to four. Doing this for five minutes helps me restore a sense of calm and presence and prepares me for what's next. Mindfulness is the state of being aware.

I recommend that you find time each day to practice mindfulness. Writing, reading, and reflecting are key to prioritizing your focus and awareness, even in the midst of all your pings, dings, and distractions.

Mindfulness Notebook

Begin or end your day with your journal or notebook. Having a practice of reflecting and writing can open you to insights. There are a lot of things you can put in this notebook:

- Capture any dreams you have.
- Write down your current feelings, aches, and pains.

- Get that to-do list out of your head and onto the page.
- Add the self-care activities you want to schedule into your day.
- Find a quote or inspirational passage that you can write in your notebook to center you.
- List one thing or person that you are grateful for.

Put the notebook aside or check it once you have completed certain tasks. Set aside fifteen minutes to reflect on how your feelings may have changed, or review your to-do list and check off every objective you have reached. When you focus on your tasks at the bookends of the day, you are more likely to be focused *throughout* the day.

Self-reflection is a necessary first step on the road to awareness. What are you currently doing to support your own mental well-being? Are you focusing only on the physical and not the mental or emotional? What is one thing that you want to begin doing that will support your well-being? You can start answering these questions now—nothing is stopping you. The answers will reveal your path and suggest any other activities that can help you cultivate the mindset you need to succeed.

Breathing and Meditation

The point of meditation is to take time to slow down. You can sit in complete silence or put on gentle music. Your mind may try to grab you, but just notice the thoughts in your head and let them go. When you meditate, your breath can be your focus—count the inhales and exhales that you take as you sit. Or, you could focus on different parts of the body. Chakras, or "wheels," are various focal points of our energetic field and used in many ancient meditation practices. They represent different energy points. Through meditation, you can focus on each chakra and bring your awareness to this part of your body. I still have a lot to learn about working with chakras The seven main chakras are:

1. **Crown Chakra (above the head):** This energy feeds your knowledge, consciousness, fulfillment, and spirituality.
2. **Third Eye Chakra (between the eyebrows):** This energy feeds your intuition, lucidity, and trust.
3. **Throat Chakra:** This energy feeds your communication, expression, creativity, and inspiration.
4. **Heart Chakra:** This energy feeds your acceptance, love, compassion, and sincerity.
5. **Solar Plexus Chakra (near the stomach):** This energy feeds your strength, personality, power, and determination.
6. **Sacral Chakra (below the navel):** This energy feeds your sensuality, sexuality, ability to appreciate pleasure, and sociability.
7. **Root Chakra (at the base of the spine):** This energy feeds your stability, comfort, and safety.

A mindful person can identify how they are feeling and where tension exists in their body. Meditating in these areas gives you all this information and more. Try it for five minutes. Try it for a few minutes. You might learn something new about yourself and your health.

Get up and Stretch

Physical movement is great, and you can still be mindful even if you're moving. If you sit at a computer for hours a day, you know how satisfying a stretch can be. Mindfully walking around the office or scheduling time to stretch every hour will help you tap into your body and come back to the present moment. Try it before a meeting. It will do wonders.

Use these tips when you're stretching mindfully:

- Stretch to a point where you feel mild tension and relax as you hold the stretch.
- If you are stretching correctly, the feeling of stretch should slightly subside as you hold the stretch. Sharp pain should be avoided. Any stretch that grows in intensity or becomes painful as you hold the stretch is an overstretch.
- Holding slow, mild stretches will identify and reduce muscle tension. Understanding where your tension lies can help you eliminate it or identify where you can focus on other self-care efforts.
- Breathe slowly, rhythmically, and under control as you stretch.
- Do not bounce.

Doing stretches is an inexpensive activity and doesn't require special equipment. They take no more than a few minutes. Just making the effort to stretch, stay mindful, and do something healthy for your body makes a significant impact. Smart decisions, great communication, and everything that makes you an excellent leader start with these small steps.

Helping Our Kids Develop Good Practices

My children are teens, and they are learning how to manage their feelings and work through frustrations. Katelyn and I were first introduced to Dr. Dweck's Growth Mindset work at our children's school. We continue to work with our kids to stay open to feedback and create opportunities for our family to hold family meetings to talk about the things that are happening in our lives, the plans for the upcoming week, and to share a "no phone zone" time together. They have so many activities and sports, plus the social whirl that has everyone moving in different directions. Helping our young ones learn Mindfulness practices—pause, take deep breathes, and relax—can help them become more aware and resourceful.

All of these small practices I offer here can be the first steps toward fostering a healthy mindset, and they start with you as a leader or a parent. Be the example.

Mindset at Worldgate

Two years ago, Katelyn and I began to understand the core values we have established for Worldgate and the culture we have built. We wanted to better articulate them so our employees really could see and understand what we wanted. This led to the creation of "Worldgate Way," twelve statements to guide behaviors, which is provided as an insert at the back of this book. It is interesting that four of them are focused on a Growth Mindset.

Open Minded: *I will be open minded to new ideas, new perspectives, and new strategies.*

Learner Mindset: *I will consistently adopt a learner mindset, so that I can be my best for my clients, team, community, and myself.*

Welcoming: *I will be welcoming to new ideas, new team members, and new clients.*

Yes...And...: *I will approach every decision and opportunity curious about the possibilities. Rather than saying "yes...but," I will reframe to "yes...and."*

What's important to us is that our employees practice being open and willing to ask for help so they can learn and grow. We encourage our employees to take time for self-care and to contribute back to their communities. Katelyn hosts a monthly online Coffee Chat and all are welcome to spend the hour in conversation. We invite curiosity and provide resources and training to support our people to take care of themselves so they can find wellbeing.

Questions for You

1. What about your current mindset moves you forward?
2. What about your current mindset holds you back?
3. What are your self-care practices?
4. Where does your mind feel most at ease?
5. How could mindfulness practices help you?

8
Leadership

"*The most powerful leadership tool you have is your own personal example.*"
—John Wooden

What is Leadership?

I define leadership as "*inspiring and motivating others toward achieving a common goal with a positive end result.*" This definition covers all of the ways that I strive to be a leader: as an entrepreneur, partner, parent, athlete, and coach.

I have been developing my leadership skills from an early age, in part because I had to take on the leadership for my own life as a teenager and young adult. Those high school experiences were part of my development, and getting positive reinforcement when my energy, interest, and relational skills set me on a productive path helped me mature.

I was fortunate to build upon this as I moved into my work at Verizon. I took on managerial responsibilities and was open to feedback from my mentors, learning from observing their own examples as strong and effective leaders. Having worked for more than 35 years, I have had a number of bosses in my life. Some of them were managers, following the direction of the leaders above them. They would tell me what to do and how to do it. They would organize our resources and manage the relationship "up" with the leaders above them.

I have also worked under senior executives who brought leadership skills to their role, as they managed their team. I found they would communicate with us, sharing the goals, objectives, and expectations for what success would require. These leaders brought their *teams* along, into a higher level of 'engagement,' in order to execute the work. My experience of those leaders, when I was fully engaged, continues to influence my *own* leadership today.

Twelve years ago, when Katelyn and I expanded Worldgate LLC beyond my real estate business into K-12 Educational Consulting and Staffing, we began hiring internal staff and recruiting and managing contractors to work onsite with our clients. Those years were a proving ground for both Katelyn and me as we established our roles and responsibilities. When you are in start-up mode, everybody does everything. There were just four of us in the office and it was an exciting and dynamic time. We were managing the needs of our young children as well as investing our time and money in making the most of the unfolding opportunities for Worldgate.

Katelyn and I brought our 'kite and 'string' dynamic into a new level. I was beginning to understand my "D" leadership style as a Driver who was action-oriented and focused on sales and implementation. Katelyn's leadership style is that of an "S," and she brought Steadiness and operational structure to our firm. In those early years, we worked hard at defining our Vision, Purpose and identifying our company's Values. These needed to align with our personal and family values, as she and I knew we were building this company to serve our family. Being married to and working with the President of the company, I knew it was crucial to up-level our communication skills.

We benefitted from engaging professional facilitation and leadership development which helped us in identifying our roles and responsibilities. Katelyn leads our financial and human resources people and she's brought her marketing experience to build our brand and establish our culture. As Chief Customer Officer, I lead sales, implementation, and client management. We lead from a clearly identified shared perspective and continue to develop our leadership skills through professional development. Our deepest commitment is to our People—those who work for us and those we work for—and our leadership styles complement one another.

Leadership development experts Dr. Jack Zenger and Dr. Joseph Folkman have identified 10 "companion behaviors that define an inspiring leader," and as leaders, Katelyn and I embrace this guidance in service to our leadership at Worldgate.

- Making the Emotional Connection
- Setting Stretch Goals
- Clear Vision
- Communication
- Developing Others
- Being Collaborative
- Being Innovative
- Taking Initiative
- Championing Change
- Being a Role Model

We now have close to seventy employees, with line managers and project managers, as well as imbedded contractors. One of the things I learned early on is that it was really important for our people to have a strong bond to Worldgate, especially because they were working in other systems that have their own culture. I am best when I get out and spend time with our managers, partners, and clients. My leadership style is relational and facilitative, and as an effective leader, I need to share our company's vision as it is aligned with our values to reach our team goals. Katelyn and I know that we need to inspire, manage, support, and empower our teams to work creatively and confidently toward that shared vision. Our people are looking to us to help them reach the next level in their career and we take this responsibility seriously. I know that to help them progress, I have to recognize where they are and what they need to change in order to grow. Some of our employees have been with the company since they were fresh out of college. Over the years, it has been rewarding to support them to become more confident in their skills, abilities, and communications.

Visionary leaders are just that—they have a vision for their lives, their companies, and the world at large. They are not blindly walking toward the end result that they want to see. They set goals and articulate their vision so others understand the desired outcomes. As I've experienced leadership at the individual level with my family and as an entrepreneur, I've found these best practices optimize a leader's impact on the organization.

Let Go of Things Others Can Do

- Delegate tasks and responsibilities that will help *others* develop by working through them.
- Know what others in the group can and want to do.
- Build up people's skills by involving them in as many tasks as they can handle.

Encourage Initiative, Creativity, and Risk-Taking

- Actively seek ideas and suggestions from your group.
- Allow people to run with an idea, even if it might involve risk.
- Reward and recognize ideas and initiative through compliments, formal recognition, and, whenever possible, tangible rewards.
- Be careful not to put down or discount ideas.

Encourage Your People

- Encourage your employees to take lead roles in setting goals and assessing their own performance.
- Make sure their goals are unambiguous and measurable.
- Let people know how they are doing in meeting their goals and offer the necessary guidance and support that they need.

Delegate to Challenge, Develop, and Empower

- Delegate authority to make decisions about the necessary work.
- Provide your delegates a clear understanding of the amount of responsibility, authority, expectations, and constraints that will accompany their new roles.
- Set up controls that keep themselves apprised of progress.

Coach to Ensure Success

- Coach employees *before* they begin their new tasks as well as *along the way* as needed.
- Make coaching a regular part of their schedule.
- Make sure all coaching sessions guide and instruct your employees while not kneecapping their self-esteem.

Reinforce Good Work and Honest Attempts at Problem-Solving

- Use verbal praise frequently.
- Know the kind of reinforcement that works best for each individual.
- Provide tangible reinforcement whenever possible (for example, recognition letters, awards, or gifts).

Share Information, Knowledge, and Skills

- Meet with your group regularly to share new information.
- Make sure that people have the information they need to succeed in their tasks and responsibilities, or make sure they know how to acquire it.

Value, Trust, and Respect Each Individual

- Show that you trust and respect your workers by encouraging them to take control of their jobs with the authority to take action.
- Take every opportunity to compliment people for good work, creative ideas, and contributions to the group.
- Listen to people and empathize with their problems and concerns.
- Be careful never to put people down or minimize their contributions.

Provide Support without Taking Over

- Understand that support is essential and know when it is needed.
- Know techniques for supporting others, such as coaching, reinforcing, preparing for resistance, and gaining others' commitment.
- Resist the temptation to take over when things go wrong.

Practice What You Preach

- Instead of punishing people for their mistakes, support them by offering them a new assignment.
- Ask your employees for ideas, but also empower them to *implement* their ideas.

Emotional Intelligence

"Leaders need strong emotional intelligence, such as empathy and interpersonal skills, to help build trust and engagement during challenging times. Being able to express empathetic concerns about difficulties helps people feel understood and shows transparency—which can restore commitment.

"Other soft skills, such as situational awareness, risk tolerance, and having a growth mindset, help leaders navigate—and even thrive—with change. They are better able to tolerate ambiguity, have greater awareness of their environments, and flex when conditions fluctuate." —Dr. Damian Vaughn, Ph.D.

Emotional intelligence (EQ) is the ability to understand and manage your emotions and those of the people around you. Emotional intelligence is essential for successful leadership. Although this sounds similar to *emotional fitness*, there are slight differences between these two terms. Emotional intelligence is the knowledge that helps you make choices related to your emotional fitness. With emotional intelligence, you have awareness and may have an easier time finding the self-care that works for you because you know what practices elevate your mood. You will show up with the right mindset more often because you have *"put on your oxygen mask first"* and can help the people around you.

Emotional intelligence has five key elements:

1. **Self-awareness:** Knowing how you feel in the moment. This knowledge illuminates your emotions *and* how they affect the people around you.
2. **Self-regulation:** Knowing how to control your behaviors when experiencing different emotions. Without self-regulation, you may make rushed decisions or stereotype people because you are unaware of how your emotions impact your thought processes. Tapping into self-regulation decreases your likelihood of verbally attacking others, making impulsive decisions, or compromising on your values because of how you feel in the moment. You know all of those regrettable decisions you make or things you say because you're overwhelmed, angry, or even hungry? Self-regulation helps you avoid them.

3. **Motivation:** The ability to work consistently toward your goals. When you are motivated, you will place higher standards on your work. Whether or not you reach those standards, you are more present and take advantage of the opportunity to learn and grow. This is crucial for personal development as well as your career. Are you motivated to understand your emotions and behaviors?

4. **Empathy:** The ability to put yourself in someone else's situation. You know how you feel, but what about your client, your colleague, or your employee? When you use empathy to develop a team, you earn respect and loyalty of everyone on the team. Through your actions, your team knows that you care and are more willing to show up and perform at their highest abilities.

5. **Social skills:** Maintaining eye contact, using proper body language, and knowing the difference between being assertive and being aggressive. Having all of these elements of emotional intelligence allows you to communicate clearly and show respect for others. This makes you a good leader and makes you someone that people want to be around.

***

One summer morning, I had a meeting that I didn't want to attend. The meeting was scheduled for 9:00 a.m. on a beautiful sunny day, and I wanted to spend that time at the beach with my family instead of indoors on a video call. I was aware that my irritation was going to be evident if I didn't do something to help reset my mood. I took five minutes to reclaim some emotional fitness by meditating. I closed my eyes and took a few deep breaths, exhaling slowly. I could feel my body relaxing and my heart rate slowing down. By the time I got on the Zoom, I was calmer. I opened space so that I could show up at this meeting with more attention and focus. My irritation set aside, the client and I made good progress, and by 9:30 a.m., the meeting was wrapped up and I was able to move on with my day at the beach.

Making that *one* choice of meditating before the meeting shifted the potential outcome and my increased self-awareness of how I want to show up—with my spouse, my children, my friends, employees, and clients—has benefitted from my learning about Emotional Intelligence. This is what leadership is all about. Emotional intelligence isn't a soft skill; it's an *essential leadership skill.*

Leaders don't develop these skills overnight. I have an inclination to make lemonade out of lemons and this reaction has contributed to my resilience throughout the years. Recently, I had an experience that brought the importance of awareness, mindfulness, and attending to my EQ into full view when triggered by stress.

In my coaching certification process, I was introduced to psychologist Daniel Goleman's work on Emotional Intelligence. In his 1995 book, *"Emotional Intelligence:*

Why It Can Matter More Than IQ," he named this emotional overreaction to stress *"amygdala hijack."* But to better understand what an amygdala hijack is, you'll need to understand a bit about how the brain functions. There are two specific parts of the brain involved in this process: the amygdala and the frontal lobes. When your amygdala responds to stress and disables your frontal lobes, it activates the fight-or-flight response and this disables rational and reasoned responses. In other words, the amygdala "hijacks" control of your brain and your responses. Anger, aggression, fear, and stress are all common emotional triggers. They can cause sudden, illogical, and even irrational reactions. An amygdala hijack may lead to inappropriate or irrational behavior and after an amygdala hijack, one may experience other symptoms like embarrassment and regret.

About eight years ago, I decided to train for a triathlon. Working out at the gym helps me clear my head and I feel stronger and clearer after I work out. But I wanted to up my game and thought that training for a triathlon, with a specific date, would increase my commitment.

It's Summer 2013 and I am set for my biggest race yet—the Eagleman Ironman 70.3. My many months of training were paying off. I'd finished the swimming portion of the race and hopped on my bike for a fifty-six-mile ride. At mile twenty-six, I took my hands off the handlebars and reached my arms over the handlebars to stretch out my lower back. By mile twenty-seven, I was told that I had been disqualified. Only later did I learn that taking your hands off the handlebars was a safety concern and strictly forbidden.

I had been training for the triathlon for months and months and in an instant, the opportunity to accomplish my goal was taken away from me. As I turned my bike around to complete my "ride of shame," back to the starting line, I found myself flooded with waves of emotion. I was angry—with the official and with myself. I was disappointed and I was also embarrassed.

I was faced with a set of choices. I could have easily grumbled and groaned my way back to my family. I could have yelled at the official. I could have looked at this triathlon in a negative light and vowed to never compete in an Ironman again. I could have considered all my training a waste. Instead, I leaned into not wanting to collapse into negativity—which is exactly what I had been training myself *not* to do during moments like this one. My mindset was well-prepared. By prioritizing my self-care and training for this triathlon, I was aware of the highjack going on in my brain and with deep breaths, and intention, I chose a positive path.

I made the deliberate decision to go to the finish line with a smile on my face. I knew my kids would see my face and be watching for my reaction. I wanted to show them how to react to adversity, better served with a smile versus a temper tantrum. I came into the staging area to pack up my gear and close out the race, I heard the winner of the race being announced: Andy Potts.

For years, I had admired Andy Potts, a professional triathlete. He's an incredibly gifted triathlete and a hero to many. Whether by fate or serendipity, he walked right by where I was packing my bike. As he walked by me, I congratulated him on his victory. I remember pointing out that we were polar opposites for this race: He had just won and I had officially lost and was one of the first to arrive back to the start after having been disqualified. He questioned what had caused my disqualification and I felt lighter when he told me he'd never heard of the rule either.

I could have easily hung my head in shame and hid from Andy, but that wasn't the way I wanted to "finish" this race. Andy was gracious and engaging, and in our brief moment together we made a connection, I took a selfie, and we continued on our way...mine to the car and his to the podium. My negative experience quickly turned into something positive that I could bring back to my family and it came from making a choice about how I handled myself.

The next year, I decided to do the triathlon again, armed with better knowledge of all the rules that could get me disqualified. I approached the event with a light heart and found the opportunity to chat with moderators, officials, and directors who had been present at the prior year's race. By remaining positive, that positivity came back to me. You get what you give, and I got more than I could have ever imagined back. An official who'd exchanged pleasantries with me the night before the race asked if my children would like to announce my heat's start. I hold the memory of my children counting down to the buzzer at the time of my heat. I will never forget the way that they yelled, *"Go, Dad, Go!"* Those voices carried me through every mile of the race, through the leg cramps, sore feet, and exhaustion. And I will never forget seeing them at the end of the race as I completed without disqualification.

Leadership is about inspiring and motivating others towards achieving a common goal, with a positive end result. Leading myself, with awareness of being aligned with my values, having empathy for myself, and setting an example for those who look to me for leadership came into full view from the seat of my bike.

Empowering the Next Generation

As long as people see the glass half full and are looking for opportunities to improve and empower themselves, I see leadership potential. As a leader I, along with Katelyn, have an important responsibility for creating and maintaining Worldgate's organizational vision. And we know we need to look ahead. What does this company seek to become in the next 5 to 10 years, and what steps are required to realize that goal? I know that an effective leader empowers others and amplifies their own impact as a result. This empowerment comes from offering formal employee training, ongoing coaching, and workforce development. Mentorship and the delegation of responsibilities helps emerging leaders to grow. Leaders must constantly be learning, and that calls for having a receptive state of mind and humility. Opportunities to learn can easily be lost if you are not willing to recognize and process mistakes. Humility also means knowing when to ask for input from others. As a young leader, if you have a gap in knowledge in a certain area, seek advice from those with more experience. Increasing your self-awareness, emotional intelligence, and conscious behaviors will help you excel as a leader, and we need you to prepare to lead in these dynamic times.

Questions for You

1. What traits do you admire most in successful leaders?
2. What are your strongest emotional skills?
3. How do you show empathy in your leadership?
4. What helps you reset yourself when under stress?
5. How do you go about transforming lemons into lemonade?

9

The Worldgate Way

"A company's culture is the foundation for future innovation. An entrepreneur's job is to build the foundation."
—Brian Chesky

In my earlier years, I enjoyed spending time in bookstores and found myself reading about entrepreneurship, real estate investing, and creating passive income. Back then, my schedule permitted hours and hours of reading these books and picking the brains of people who were living the life I wanted to live. This helped inspire me on my path toward financial independence and the kind of career that I envisioned for myself.

The original purpose for Worldgate was as a real estate holding company. The money I made and saved was invested into building Worldgate. We made a big shift in 2009 and that set the groundwork for the firm we are today. I became a consultant because I had developed relationships with people who needed help and their needs were services I knew how to provide. My skills aren't solely in technology, and I hadn't worked much in education before Worldgate. I didn't need to possess the required technical skills. I could hire others who had them. I was able to help the people who I had business relationships with solve their problems. I explored how K-12 school districts implemented IT solutions. Institutional leadership struggled with who would manage this project. HR? IT? Finance? In-house staff at a school district was unable to take it on. The employees were already stretched too thin and time constraints prevented them from completing these big projects in a timely manner.

This was a recurring problem for school districts, and what's worse is, they didn't know where to turn. Large consulting firms were the primary companies available to deliver these enterprise solutions. The big firms tried to push for resources and expensive packages that didn't always solve the problems that school districts were trying to solve. And these projects were being funded by taxpayer dollars. Leaders in school districts that I had connected with started asking me for advice. *"How do we put the pieces together to implement these solutions?"*

I was very clear when I had these conversations. I could advocate, but I couldn't deliver a huge technological solution with thousands of laptops or the perfect software program that these huge firms embedded into their proposals. What Worldgate *could do* was position itself to be the consulting project manager and resource manager that K-12 leadership had been so desperately looking for. In time, we would train and hand the project over to their managers who could then monitor and maintain the systems.

Essentially, Worldgate was built to partner with clients to complete the due diligence they needed to deploy and operate their IT organizations. School districts seemed to love this idea. They didn't have to find a manager to figure everything out about their new IT systems, and they would pay a fraction of the price that huge consulting firms were proposing. Worldgate had found its way into this niche, and from there, we had plenty of room to grow.

Worldgate's first consulting RFP was awarded. A school district submitted a request for proposal to help them train and deliver a new technology. When I showed up and provided effective training for our first client, suddenly people throughout the school district started calling my personal cell phone. Worldgate was small, nimble, and responsive.

In time we were able to step up to the plate for larger contracts as our processes weren't over-manufactured and we had demonstrated expertise in the K-12 space. We paid close attention to our clients' procurement vehicles and registered so they could procure our services more easily. We continued to recruit and train talent and our clients appreciated the certifications we obtained. This was a new niche we were excited to start serving. This awareness and nimble approach paid off, because huge consulting firms suddenly began to see the value in our services and in turn would offer us opportunities to subcontract with them. They were inhibited by regulations, corporate criteria, and high overhead. Worldgate wasn't. And as word got around about our growing potential in the industry, consultants from these larger companies started to send their resumes to us.

Stepping Up

As Worldgate attracted more and more clients, I envisioned where we could go and how we could grow. I wanted more than what we were doing and knew that we could fulfill a greater potential because we were hiring great people. I couldn't empower my team by playing small, and I knew every one of my team members could do so much more than manage an implementation. I turned to my business coach. Worldgate's biggest asset was our ability to bring in the right resources at a lower price than our competitors. But how else could we add value?

Our Strategic Advisors worked with us to do a thorough SWOT Analysis to help us understand our organizational Strengths and Weaknesses, as well as external Opportunities and Threats. We looked at the competitive field we were working in, the dynamics of the economy, and what it would require to build a strategy to grow the company. We determined where Katelyn and I wanted to take Worldgate and what obstacles might be in our way. Building a vision for how Worldgate would fit into our lives as parents and business partners, we decided to step up our game and offer more than just staffing and recruiting services. We wanted to become a better systems integrator. This is what Worldgate is today.

Certifying Our Processes

In a short period of time, I wanted to strengthen our processes and began exploring the benefits of earning an International Organization Standardization (ISO) certification. This certification sends a specific message to clients and other companies that we meet international standards with proven methodologies. Specifically, the ISO 9001:2015 ISO certification demonstrated that we had met specific requirements for a quality management system that enhanced customer satisfaction.

I engaged the one person I knew who had the experience and could kick things off effectively in our start-up: my father. Dad's efforts and experience managing my task team landed us an audited certification—ISO 9001 certified. With this certification, clients no longer had to "take our word for it." By 2013, this certification displayed clearly to our customers that Worldgate was solidly established in the market. With an experienced workforce to follow through on all of the processes that we had certified, we were still committed to continue offering our services at a competitive rate. Our fees were already much lower than big-name firms, and our bench of experience, drive, and credibility were now on par with them. Our team, our processes, and our pricing were the puzzle pieces that, when put together, have formed the vision that I had drawn up for Worldgate.

Building Relationships

Every step we took to cement Worldgate's position in the industry was supported by relationships. People from all chapters of my life came together to support Worldgate as it started. Relationships formed as Worldgate ebbed and flowed, until individuals and companies found their place within Worldgate. Relational maintenance is crucial for entrepreneurs who are starting a business. Not everyone is going to be readily available to help you as you build your vision or work with your first clients, and that's OK. Keep them around. Know these relationships may fit in the present, or maybe they will fit in the future. You never know where these relationships will end up as your business grows and transforms.

There is no better example of this than an early-years' relationship we had implementing Kronos human capital management technology software for one of our early clients. The implementation was successful, and we were excited to continue to partner with Kronos as our company grew. Unfortunately, the decision was made to move in a different direction away from Kronos. The split was bittersweet, as Worldgate had enjoyed the experience, so we parted ways cordially.

Roughly five years later, Worldgate had further established and expanded in the K-12 space. We were a force to be reckoned with in the niche we served. I began using social media to promote our happenings, recent successes, and employee/client experiences. I shared updates on LinkedIn about implementations, our work at various school districts, highlighting customers and introducing our project managers, business analysts, production support specialists, and contractors. Social media has been great in helping us share what we are doing in the K-12 space.

Social media also brought us back into conversations with Kronos, which had recently merged with another firm and changed their name to Ultimate Kronos Group (UKG). One of their leaders, Linda, reached out to say she had been following Worldgate stories on LinkedIn and were impressed by our progress in the K-12 space. UKG had undergone similar growth during that time and our paths were finally ready to cross again. In fact, we agreed that Worldgate would be their exclusive partner in the K-12 space. Remember earlier when I shared our decision to offer more than just staffing and recruiting services? Our decision to become a systems integrator was the service they sought.

This conversation wasn't just a huge step forward for Worldgate, it proved once again, to me, there is serendipity in maintaining great relationships. Everything I had been doing as a leader, taking the steps to make Worldgate visible by sharing our success on social media, had led to this moment. Kronos appreciated not only our growth, but our ISO-certified business practices and our cost-effectiveness. I got a kick out of seeing how the puzzle pieces fit so well.

By 2021, we had implemented UKG's technology in roughly forty school districts and our partnership is now an entire division of our company. We have gone from one Worldgate member focused on this division to fifteen employees and almost doubling the number of customers we can take on in the future.

Win-Win Networking

I love this story of Worldgate partnering effectively to meet the needs of our clients while helping the next generation of students. When the COVID-19 pandemic hit we had to make major adjustments, as every business did. Our employees were needing to work remotely and our K-12 clients were having to make significant modifications to deliver solutions through their IT department.

Just months into the pandemic, we opened a hotline for the parents at one of our premier school district clients. This was meant to help parents and students get Chromebooks expeditiously as online learning was now the new norm. Our district client selected us to set up the hotline because they knew that they could rely on us to take a nimble and progressive approach to deal with this innovation at such an uncertain time.

The importance of relationships played a significant role in our success. I recruited many friends and colleagues to help refer potential candidates to staff the Hotline and answer parents' calls. I'd developed my relationship with Pat years before at Verizon, and we had stayed connected. I reached out to her for help with staffing the help line. Pat recommended that we recruit Broadway actors who were now out-of-work since Broadway had shut down due to COVID-19. Pat's son, Frank, is a leader in the NYC media and acting community and he helped connect us to the Actors Fund[1] who in turn helped us recruit potential actors who were willing to work and were available.

Thanks to the network, personal and business connections, we were ultimately able to onboard about seventy-five contractors in less than two weeks. These workers supported the dissemination of about eighty-thousand Chromebooks across the school district. They instructed parents on where to pick them up, as well as how to repair them if they broke. The actors were grateful for the income, and with their professional backgrounds, they got the job done with energy, ease, and minimal training. The one-page script that kicked things off became a 100-page manual for new hires and the Chromebooks hotline continues to help parents, students, and teachers stay connected through these challenging times.

I never would have been able to recruit such an amazing and diverse crew of experienced people—now hotline workers—if I hadn't kept my network alive. It reinforced my commitment to nurturing my relationships, communicating effectively, and remaining

---

[1] "Entertainment Community Fund," Entertainment Community Fund, n.d., https://actorsfund.org/.

calm and nimble during uncertain times. I'm proud that the Worldgate team was able to meet the ever-shifting demands of our clients during the challenges of the COVID-19 pandemic.

Recognition and Rewards

Worldgate has always been a company with a purpose. We serve our clients well, but what's more, we serve our communities well, too. Our efforts have included feeding hungry students, providing school supplies, and reading to children in the classroom. In return, we received the 2019 Virginia School Boards Association Business Honor Roll award. We were selected as one of the top three from 400 submittals from our community.

We are also proud to have received many accolades and recognition over the years. Some we like to highlight include the 2017 BRAVA Award, the 2018 Mid-Atlantic Women's Leadership Award, UKG White Glove Partner of the Year in 2021, and our coveted *INC Magazine* "5000 Fastest Growing Companies of America" in 2021 and 2022. Worldgate ranked 248 in Virginia and 3,948 Nationally in 2021. Recently, The Washington Post recognized us for Top Places to Work 2022 as well. We appreciate the recognition we receive for our success, and it inspires us to do more and continue to give to our employees and communities. It's the Worldgate Way.

***

In 2020, Worldgate was growing and solidifying its processes as a systems integrator. But as the business grew, my leaders came to me asking for the "why." Clients knew what we did, and they knew that we could do it well. The "what" of our company was solid, but the "why" was eluding our employees and wasn't spelled out well for our clients or community either. Why did we insist on going above and beyond to obtain an ISO certification? Why did we make choices that kept us afloat as K-12 schools suffered economic highs and lows? Why did we set our prices the way that we did? How did we integrate our mission-based work with for-profit work?

Before the implementation of Worldgate Way, Katelyn and I assumed that all our employees understood the values we wanted to promote. Katelyn and I could answer these questions ourselves because we understood each other and the business. The rest of the team wasn't as dialed into Worldgate's culture as we were. One day, one of our managers finally asked us, "What *is* Worldgate Way?" We had thought that our values were already embedded in our culture, but we realized that we needed to articulate them. Worldgate cultural behaviors couldn't just be inferred; they had to be explicitly communicated and available in trainings, on our website, and to anyone who wanted to know more about our company. It had to be something that people recognized in us because we intentionally lived it, day in and day out, for years.

The Worldgate Way

The Worldgate Way are values and behaviors that we promote so we achieve the success that we envision for our company, our employees, and our clients. It consists of twelve letters, which spell out "Worldgate Way:"

W: Willing

I will be willing to do the work, strive for excellence, take on new initiatives, share my ideas, and admit when I am wrong.

O: Open-Minded

I will be open-minded to new ideas, new perspectives, and new strategies.

R: Responsive

I will be responsive to clients and team members.

L: Learner Mindset

I will consistently adopt a learner mindset, so I can be the best for my clients, team, community, and myself.

D: Diversity

I will respect diversity of race, gender, sexual orientation, ethnicity, and perspective, as that diversity, equity, and inclusion drives excellence.

G: Generous

I will be generous with my time, knowledge, and compassion in the workplace. I will strive to be generous in the spirit of giving back to my community.

A: Accountable

I will be accountable for getting the job done in a timely and high-quality manner. I will continuously think about how things could be done better. I will admit when I am wrong and will be willing to make amends.

T: Thoughtful

I will be thoughtful in all that I do, from strategic, tactical, and empathetic standpoints.

E: Ethical

I will always be ethical, conducting myself in accordance with the rules of law and standards of right conduct set forth by my employer and clients.

W: Welcoming

I will be welcoming to new ideas, new team members, and new clients.

A: Adaptable

I will adapt and excel when priorities shift and strategies evolve.

Y: Yes. . .and. . .

I will approach every decision and opportunity curious about the possibilities. Rather than saying, "Yes. . .but," I will reframe to "Yes. . .and."

We're Unconventional—and It Works

Expressing our culture through the Worldgate Way may seem unconventional, but it works for us. Plus, our ability to be unconventional has enormous benefits when we are working directly with clients. Worldgate has been able to navigate a specific niche in ways that larger consulting firms often cannot. Advantages like this have also shaped our ability to create and build our company culture.

Take "Yes, and. . ." No, we're not an improv group. "Yes, and. . ." doesn't mean you always have to say the words, "Yes, and." This value refers to *looking for other possibilities.* Conversations shut down when team members respond to ideas with, "Yes, but. . ." or "No." No one will speak up in meetings if they believe they are going to get shut down. Clients walk away when they hear "No," because they assume another firm will say, "Yes."

I've seen when working in a larger consulting firm, you do have to say "No." You can't embody "Yes, and. . ." as a value because it's not always possible when you're in a larger infrastructure. The restrictions and regulations of a larger company can sometimes hold team members back from looking for possibilities, especially if they are unconventional. That's not what Worldgate is about.

For us, "Yes, and. . ." means that we can work with our customers in an unconventional way. We can be flexible in our partnership and switch gears on a dime. If we see the solution in our "Yes, and. . ." we can pivot to it.

By communicating this to our team, we empower them to explore the "Yes, and. . ." They know this is a move that they can make because it's so ingrained in the company culture. Not only is "Yes, and. . ." allowed, it's expected.

Writing down this series of cultural behaviors has increased our effectiveness as leaders. All of us can now speak about our culture through the Worldgate Way. Every person that walks through our doors is given information about how our culture is core to our business. They know what to expect because they can look at the Worldgate Way and we encourage them to act on it every day. We live these behaviors. If team members have difficulty embracing these behaviors, they are offered more training and support. If they don't want to learn, embody, and execute these behaviors, we respectfully recommend they work for another company. Not every person is willing to grasp our mission and play it out in their daily responsibilities, but if they can, we want them on our team.

Applying the Worldgate Way

Once these behaviors were established, we sent everyone at Worldgate tent cards with all the behaviors of Worldgate Way written on them. We also launched multiple programs that encourage these behaviors in and out of the office. I truly believe that words are defined by their action, not by the word itself. At Worldgate, we act on our behaviors every single day.

Every month, we seek nominations from our teams on who is manifesting Worldgate Way in their daily life at work. Because there are twelve distinct behaviors in Worldgate Way, each month highlights a different behavior. In January, we emphasize "willingness," in February, we emphasize "open-mindedness," etc. People can nominate peers, managers, or direct reports whom they feel demonstrate that month's behavior.

We want our team to really *live* these behaviors, and we recognize them even when it's outside of Worldgate business. When we highlighted "Generosity" in June 2020, we asked for nominations. Three people nominated the same team member for his work outside of Worldgate. This particular employee works tirelessly rehabilitating prisoners, and yet he never misses a meeting with his team at Worldgate. It doesn't matter that he's being nominated for his work outside of Worldgate. We designed the Worldgate Way culture behaviors and reward system to be applied in the same way. This particular team member is a true leader and extremely generous with his time, so much so that employees said he embodied the cultural value of generosity.

Highlighting great work is more than just giving someone a pat on the back. Through this program, we promote our culture, how we give back to the community, and how every single person can embody the behaviors that we have established with the Worldgate Way. We encourage managers to talk about Worldgate Way with their teams and their clients. All our clients know that we expect our employees to work with them, using these cultural behaviors. Feedback, from our clients, helps us reinforce and reward how the Worldgate Way is influencing our employees to deliver their best. In addition to the recognition program, we also ensure that Worldgate leadership embodies these behaviors as part of their managerial responsibilities.

We knew we had to do more than *just talk* about generosity. Recognizing a person who embodies generosity gives people an example of how to be generous. We wanted to take this one step further and decided to provide resources to do so through Worldgate. At the holidays, we gave all our employees a gift card to donate to a nonprofit of their choice. We provided resources so each of our employees could contribute to their communities. Everyone was able to give in their own way. Some people chose to donate to a local food bank; others chose a charity that was closer to their hearts. In and outside of the workplace, we encourage our team members to act with generosity.

The feedback we received was remarkable. Our team loved it. Our colleagues and connections loved it too when we posted about the initiative on social media. We've recently learned that other companies are adopting the same practice with their teams.

Offering a gift card to every employee doesn't break the bank for Worldgate, we budget for it each year. However, it does make a serious impact on our clients, partners, teams, and recipients. Our actions "walk the walk" and clients, employees, and communities appreciate that. Employees recognize the ways we live our company culture, and we benefit from having very high retention and employee satisfaction. Company culture isn't *fluffy stuff*—it's foundational to what makes Worldgate a great place to work.

Questions for You

1. What values and behaviors do you want to define for your business?
2. How can you communicate these behaviors effectively?
3. How could articulating your culture support your company's success?
4. What companies have you worked for or researched whose culture impacted you?
5. What is the greatest lesson you are taking away from this story?

Final Thoughts

Your story is the greatest legacy that you can leave to your friends.
It is the longest lasting legacy you will leave to your heirs."
—Steve Saint

Founding Worldgate was never *just* about seeking financial success. I built this company because I had set goals for myself. I wanted to have enough financial stability *and* enough time to raise my three children *and* be a good husband to my wife. Understanding these goals built the vision for Worldgate: a company that acted on its compassionate culture, not just talked about it. After the hierarchy of needs has been met, I'm interested in offering a significant portion of Worldgate's resources to be shared with employees and the community. In the same way that I build lifelong relationships with people I work with, I want our employees to regard each other as potential bonus family members. Certainly, having a clearly established culture makes it explicit for all stakeholders to see, and that's how my career has always worked. How I live my life supports how I approach my career, and how I approach my career supports how I live my life. That's how I got here, by committing to the same values using and improving on the same skills everywhere I go.

I hope that throughout the journey of reading this book, you understand—and perhaps even relate—to how important all of this has been to me. Everything— from partnership and relationships, habits, mindset, and self-care to building a company culture—ties it all together. While there are certainly other scenarios to drive home these concepts, these were the ones I felt compelled to share as a cursory start for any young man or woman launching or revamping their careers. The lessons I've learned from my coaches and mentors exposed me to these—and so many other—crucial strategies and skills. When I've applied them, I've done bigger and better things in my life and business. I feel more fulfilled, find more value in each day, and I find myself in places that I would have never dreamt of reaching.

Katelyn and I have built a beautiful life together. As my wife, partner, and friend, I am here today, and grateful, because she's been—and still is—the "string" to my "kite." Our children, Evan, Teddy, and Phoebe are our hearts and truly, our finest achievement. We have been driven to provide for our kids so they have financial stability, a safe and secure home life, are able to enjoy family vacations at the beach and not have to worry about funding their educations. We want our kids to feel empowered to build lives that fulfill them and appreciate all the options that are available to them. May they also remember how important gratitude is and to pay it forward.

What do you dream about doing? Becoming a parent? Getting a promotion? Pursuing creative endeavors? Do you dream of starting a company? I hope this book has offered you "food for thought" and you've been able to take the time to think about your vision and how to start taking the steps to follow it. Your goals will change and evolve as you recognize where your life's opportunities are taking you. That's OK, as long as you continue to learn and grow from your experiences.

Even as I finish this book, I am looking forward. Building Worldgate has been the end goal for many years, and we have reached many of the milestones that I set. I look forward to completing my bachelor's degree from the University of Virginia in 2023, as that has been a long pursuit. My early college experiences, like my early life, were somewhat disjointed. Yet, *all things do happen in the right time.* So, with appreciation to my parents and the life they gave me, I leave you now and look ahead with curiosity, purpose, and potential.

Working with Worldgate

Worldgate's Strategic Advisory Services (SAS) practice leverages the entire firm's technology experience, cross-functional capabilities, and market knowledge to enable successful strategy-driven approaches. Our professionals can assist at every stage of an IT program, from business strategy and architecture design to program transformation and infrastructure integration, to increased operational efficiency. Our skills include focusing on studying the application of emerging technologies and the practice-wide discipline in applying analytical techniques to identify and measure business-value drivers that enable our team to deliver innovative, high-value, technical service offerings.

In today's challenging business environment, IT professionals must consider much more than just technology software and service providers. They manage IT across entire organizations and keep businesses running efficiently and cost-effectively amid regulatory changes, market opportunities, and business planning. An organization's success depends on IT delivering tangible value-creation for the business. Clients engage our teams to support various programs of this kind of work, including headhunting, project management, business analysts, and production support that all assist with software implementation and rolling out enterprise-wide execution programs.

Our Approach

Strategy and Architecture

Our strategy team works with clients to improve the business value gained from investments in technology and operations. They also work to align technology initiatives with their business strategy and transformation agendas. We collaborate with our clients' senior executive teams and management to identify key business drivers and to define actionable strategies and roadmaps to achieve value-based outcomes. We use our team's deep IT and operational competencies to develop strategies and roadmaps that support our clients' agendas and deliver the desired business outcomes. We work with IT and operations leadership to address their critical delivery agendas. We offer what their employees need to do their jobs.

Infrastructure and Operations

Our team helps align, prioritize, and deliver what is most critical to our client's business. We assist our clients with optimizing their core IT infrastructure and operational functions by leveraging industry-leading, ISO-certified processes and practices. We can help our clients deliver risk-based infrastructure services to create transparency around cost management and performance while increasing efficiency. Our offerings focus on IT value creation and delivery capability. Our combination of experience, knowledge, and a risk-based approach provides an end-to-end capability for the entire IT ecosystem, creating the opportunity for business and IT to perform as a seamlessly integrated entity.

Transformation and Integration

Our Transformation and Integration team drives the planning, execution, and monitoring of transformative initiatives in businesses and technology, leveraging deep delivery knowledge and industry-leading, ISO-certified methods. We facilitate required change within client organizations, offering a range of services. We can also guide strategic initiatives to help achieve business objectives, reduce risk, and enable long-term success. Our initiatives include:

- Development of complex RFPs
- Creation and maintenance of strategic technology roadmaps
- Technology risk assessments
- Presentations and meetings with non-IS executives for assistance in demonstration of value of IT deployments
- Facilitation of IS management meetings/workshops

Services

IT Strategy Development

Our IT Strategy Development includes an integrated and business aligned IT strategy framework, supported by comprehensive methodologies, and a range of tools and project accelerators. Our framework has been successfully used to develop several strategies and implement roadmaps for a wide spectrum of public sector and K-12 organizations.

Strategic Advisory

Working with a Worldgate Strategic Advisor helps clients move their technology organization forward by addressing the following five key areas: strategy, productivity, risk management, talent development, and reporting.

Strategy

We help clients answer the question, "Are we doing the right things?" We work with clients to develop and implement a strategy that aligns and optimizes investments in people, process, and technology. Typical focus areas include the following:

- Business and IT strategy alignment
- IT steering committee management
- Monthly recurring advisor sessions
- Policies and procedures implementation
- Key relationships development
- Sounding board for key decision-making
- Technical action plan assistance
- Project reviews and business case development

Productivity

We help you answer the question, "Are we doing things right?" Our experienced advisors help clients' organizations better integrate technology into their business processes and pinpoint opportunities for them to do more with less. Typical focus areas include:

- Process automation
- Technology enablement
- Benchmarking
- KPI (Key Performance Indicator) development and measurement

Risk Management

We implement processes to help ensure that IT systems remain effective and secure, increasing consistency, transparency, and accountability throughout clients' technology organizations. Our team can help reduce risk and subsequently drive enhanced business value and satisfaction with IT through:

- IT governance design and implementation
- Disaster recovery planning
- Business continuity planning
- Monitoring and incident response

Talent Development

Our advisors are seasoned technology professionals with extensive leadership experience. We can help clients' organizations attract, develop, and retain high-performing IT staff. Typical focus areas include:

- Skills assessments
- IT organization design
- Roles and responsibilities
- IT leadership development
- Mentoring and coaching programs

Decision-Making

Our advisors can implement technology strategies that make the most of clients' data to promote more effective business decisions. We can help clients develop a comprehensive data foundation to provide deeper insight and analytics through:

- Leadership progress reports
- Executive committee meetings
- Ongoing executive communications and updates

Worldgate's comprehensive strategic advisory services supplement a client organization's technology leadership, providing advice and experience that may not be available from in-house staff. A Worldgate strategic advisor helps align a client's people, process, and technology with the strategic goals of the business to create and deliver a cohesive and innovative organizational strategy. Our advisors understand a client's challenges, and they oversee the development and implementation of an IT roadmap, working with key business stakeholders to address mutually defined and agreed-upon IT initiatives.

This is the market niche that Worldgate continues to fill.

Acknowledgments

First, I'd like to acknowledge my wife, Katelyn, and our children, Evan, Teddy, and Phoebe, without whom I would not have strength in times of weakness, or love in times of despair.

Thank you, Mom and Dad and Dan, for your support and unconditional love.

Love to all my friends during my high school and early college years, many of whom I'm still in touch with today. Notables are Tammy, Karen, Frank, Sharon, Brian, Joe, Colin, Tom/Denise and Kate/Matt. These people have influenced my life in so many special and unique ways. It's a wonderful life with all of you in it. Special shout out to parents Becky & Frank Sr. and Kathy P. for your incredible familial support during those early years.

Thanks to all my leaders, managers, and colleagues while I worked at Bell Atlantic Business Supplies, InfoSpeed, and later Verizon, many of whom I still talk with, spend time with, and call my friends. Special recognition to Jim K., Bill J., and Amy E. for always looking out for me and supporting that life changing decision to send me south. Lastly, Jimmy, you instigated the biggest game changer to come out of those years by repeatedly tickling the notion that I ask Katelyn out on a date. Twenty-six years later and you are the ultimate match maker.

Everyone needs friends who are walking similar life and career paths. I'm not sure that Worldgate would have ever launched when it did if I hadn't had that fateful dinner at Big Bowl with Chris, Matt, and Jeff. I believe everyone needs friends who are walking similar life or career paths and who support you unconditionally. Over the decades these gentlemen—including Jeff S. from Gold's—have been there for me offering connections, invaluable insight, trust, encouragement, and brotherly love. *Wolfpacks* are important.

Nothing but heart for my dear friends Rob and Kelly. The deep connection we have established with our families is immeasurable. I am truly honored to have my children all but adopt you as their aunt and uncle and our children all intermingle as if they were cousins. You all truly define what it means to be f-*r*-amily.

Special recognition to Worldgate's longest-tenured employees Justin and Tinsley. These two exemplify the learner mindset and continue to offer their support and encouragement. I am grateful and honored to have had a front row seat to such amazing growth and career progression over the past ten plus years.

To all Worldgate leadership, management, employees, and contractors, all of your efforts, contribution, and loyalty are not lost on us. Katelyn's and my gratitude knows no limit.

Thanks to Logan of Lion's Pen and Gretchen of Process Experts for your never-ending support interviewing, editing, and helping me compile the data and documents that led to this book. Further, the teams of Leaders Press, some of whom forged ahead through serious despair, while others tolerated my lack of experience with writing a book. I hope you will agree the end result is something we can all be proud of.

These people are all significant contributors to

HOW I GOT HERE!

Love for All.

Thank you, readers, for picking up this book and indulging the anecdotes and experiences. Hopefully you find them presented in a way that they help you succeed in finding your happiness.

Who is Scott Montgomery?

Scott Montgomery is Wall Street Journal, USA Today, and Amazon bestselling author for his contribution to *Success Mindsets*. He is responsible for overseeing the day-to-day operations, consulting services, and sales teams of Worldgate, LLC. He is greatly focused on nurturing the growth of Worldgate's employees, our client relationships, and strategic alliances, including Worldgate's important alliance with Ultimate Kronos Group.

Despite many certifications and leadership training accomplishments, Scott deferred obtaining his bachelor's degree for building the business. In May 2020, Scott was accepted by the admission department of the University of Virginia (UVA) to pursue his degree. He looks forward at the time of this writing to graduating with a Bachelor of Liberal Arts in May 2023. Scott previously earned an Associate of Science (AS) degree with honors (Phi Theta Kappa) from Northern Virginia Community College and is excited to finalize this personal bucket-list item from UVA.

Scott's leadership approach starts with employee well-being, growth, and fostering a learner mindset. He completed George Mason University's certification program as a certified leadership and organizational well-being coach and has achieved and since renewed an ICF-ACC accreditation. Scott is proud to lead an amazing team that collaborates with awesome clients and looks forward to many more years of service to the public sector industry Worldgate serves.

Scott's priority is his family. He is a loving husband of over twenty years and a proud, hands-on father of three teens, including twins. He enjoys long walks with his wife and loves varying pursuits of physical fitness. He has completed more than fifteen Sprint and Olympic-sized triathlons, as well as an Ironman 70.3. He aspires to do a full Ironman one day and hopes to continue indulging in his earned happiness.

Willing
I will be **willing** to do the work, strive for excellence, take on new initiatives, share my ideas, and admit when I am wrong.

Generous
I will be **generous** with my time, knowledge and compassion in the workplace. I will strive to be generous in the spirit of giving back to my community.

Open Minded
I will be **open minded** to new ideas, new perspectives, and new strategies.

Welcoming
I will be **welcoming** to new ideas, new team members and new clients.

Responsive
I will be **responsive** to clients and team members.

Accountable
I will be **accountable** for getting the job done in a timely and high-quality manner. I will continuously think about how things could be done better. I will admit when I am wrong and will be willing to make amends.

Adaptable
I will **adapt** and excel when priorities shift and strategies evolve.

Learner Mindset
I will consistently adopt a **learner mindset**, so that I can be the best for my clients, team, community and myself.

Thoughtful
I will be **thoughtful** in all that I do, from strategic, tactical and empathetic standpoints.

Yes… And…
I will approach every decision and opportunity curious about the possibilities. Rather than saying "yes…but," I will reframe to **"yes…and."**

Diverse
I will respect **diversity** of race, gender, sexual orientation, ethnicity and perspective, as that diversity, equity, and inclusion drives excellence.

Ethical
I will always be **ethical**, conducting myself in accordance with the rules of law and standards of right conduct set forth by my employer and clients.

worldgate WAY

worldgate™

GAIN MORE WISDOM FOR YOUR JOURNEY.

Follow Scott Montgomery's latest insights, tools, and teachings at **HowDidYouGetHere.com**, as you pursue your goals and forge your own unique path to greater success.

▶ **Sign up to stay driven.**

Visit **HowDidYouGetHere.com** and download our **FREE** goal-setting guide — to help you get to your next milestone.